EMBEDDED DEEP LEARNING

&

GENERATIVE AI ALGORITHMS

Table of Contents:

1. Introduction to Embedded Deep Learning and Generative AI

2. Foundations of Deep Learning

3. Introduction to Generative AI

4. Hardware for Embedded Deep Learning

5. Software Frameworks and Tools

6. Design and Optimization of Deep Learning Models

7. Implementation of Generative AI Models

8. Case Studies in Embedded Deep Learning

9. Ethical Considerations and Challenges

10. Future Trends in Embedded Deep Learning and Generative AI

11. Appendices

Structure of the Book

Embedded deep learning & generative AI algorithms offer a systematic exploration of deep learning and generative artificial intelligence within embedded systems, meticulously crafted to equip readers with theoretical foundations and applied expertise. Structured as a progressive intellectual journey, the text methodically shepherds readers from elementary principles to sophisticated implementations while addressing the nuanced complexities inherent in resource-constrained environments. Bringing abstract algorithmic frameworks with pragmatic engineering considerations fosters a pedagogical synergy between innovation and practicality, underscored by case studies and industry-relevant scenarios illuminating the intersection of cutting-edge AI and embedded architectures. The treatise prioritizes not only conceptual mastery but also the cultivation of problem-solving acumen, preparing practitioners to navigate the evolving landscape of intelligent systems design amidst real-world constraints. The following is an overview of the book's structure, outlining the main topics and themes covered in each chapter.

Chapter 1: Introduction

This introductory chapter sets the stage for the entire book. It begins with an overview of deep learning and generative AI, highlighting their importance and impact across various industries. The chapter then delves into the specific challenges associated with implementing these technologies in embedded environments. Finally, the structure of the book is outlined, providing readers with a roadmap of what to expect in the subsequent chapters.

Chapter 2: Fundamentals of Deep Learning

Chapter 2 focuses on the foundational concepts of deep learning. It covers the basics of neural networks, including their architecture, activation functions, and training processes. Key topics such as backpropagation, optimization algorithms, and loss functions are explained in detail. The chapter also introduces different types of neural networks, including convolutional neural networks (CNNs) and recurrent neural networks (RNNs), providing a solid grounding for understanding more advanced concepts in later chapters.

Chapter 3: Generative AI Techniques

In this chapter, the focus shifts to generative AI. The fundamental principles of generative modeling are explained, along with an overview of the most prominent generative models, such as Generative Adversarial Networks (GANs) and Variational Autoencoders (VAEs). The chapter explores how these models work, their applications, and the challenges associated with training and deploying them. Practical examples and case studies illustrate the power and versatility of generative AI.

Chapter 4: Deep Learning in Embedded Systems

Chapter 4 addresses the specific challenges and strategies for implementing deep learning in embedded systems. It discusses hardware constraints, model optimization techniques, and the use of specialized hardware accelerators like GPUs, TPUs, and NPUs. The chapter also covers software frameworks and tools that facilitate the deployment of deep learning models on embedded devices. Real-world examples demonstrate how these concepts are applied in practice.

Chapter 5: Generative AI in Embedded Systems

Building on the previous chapter, Chapter 5 explores the integration of generative AI into embedded systems. It examines the unique challenges posed by generative models in resource-constrained environments and discusses techniques for optimizing and deploying these models. The chapter also highlights practical applications of generative AI in embedded systems, such as synthetic data generation, content creation, and personalization.

Chapter 6: Applications in Various Industries

Chapter 6 provides an in-depth look at how deep learning and generative AI are transforming different industries. It covers applications in healthcare, automotive, finance, entertainment, retail, manufacturing, environmental sustainability, and education. Each section includes detailed case studies and examples, showcasing the impact of these technologies and the solutions to industry-specific challenges.

Chapter 7: Advanced Topics and Emerging Trends

This chapter explores advanced topics and emerging trends in deep learning and generative AI. It discusses cutting-edge research areas such as neuromorphic computing, edge AI, and the convergence of AI with blockchain and quantum computing. The chapter also examines the ethical considerations and societal impacts of AI, including bias, privacy, and transparency. Readers are encouraged to think critically about the future direction of AI technologies and their implications.

Chapter 8: Practical Implementation

Chapter 8 provides a hands-on guide to implementing deep learning and generative AI in embedded systems. It includes step-by-step instructions for setting up development environments, training and deploying models, and optimizing performance. The chapter covers practical tools and libraries, such as TensorFlow Lite, ONNX, and PyTorch Mobile, and offers tips and best practices for successful implementation.

Chapter 9: Case Studies and Real-World Examples

To bring theory into practice, Chapter 9 presents a series of detailed case studies and real-world examples. These case studies highlight successful implementations of deep learning and generative AI in various embedded applications, discussing the challenges faced, solutions developed, and outcomes achieved. This chapter serves as an inspiration and reference for readers looking to apply the concepts learned in their own projects.

Chapter 10: Future Directions and Conclusion

The final chapter reflects on the current state of deep learning and generative AI in embedded systems and looks ahead to future developments. It discusses ongoing research, potential breakthroughs, and the evolving landscape of AI technologies. The chapter concludes with a summary of key takeaways and encourages readers to continue exploring and innovating in this dynamic field.

Chapter 1: Introduction to Embedded Deep Learning and Generative AI

1.1 Overview of Deep Learning & Generative AI

From the technologies, the deep learning (DL) as well as generative artificial intelligence (AI) may transform the performance of different sectors. These are branches, or areas of functioning, that employ ANN with more than one layer for pattern recognition in data; deep learning is a subcategory and niche of machine learning. Another branch of AI is generative AI and its task includes producing new data based on the learned data. Altogether the technologies are making it more and more important for progresses in nearly all the spheres starting from the Healthcare, Automotive Industry, Finances and ending with entertainment and making it difficult to distinguish between machines and what they are capable of doing.

In its most basic form, deep learning is founded on the structure as well as the operation of the human brain. An artificial neural network, the fundamental of deep learning is a conjunction of layers of nodes or neurons. It also possesses a weight and during training the weight is adjusted in the reciprocal with its error in relation to the forecast made. The above-mentioned learning process known as backpropagation empowers deep learning models to learn about the representations of data. That is why the depth of these networks, which is defined as the number of layers, helps to detect hierarchal patterns and is suitable for such tasks as image and speech recognition or natural language processing and others.

Comparing these two versions of AI, generative AI is significantly more complex than the previous kinds, as it not only analyses and recognizes data but also predicts it. It aims at creating new data from the training data set belonging to the same data type.

What is more nerve-racking is its potentiality: It does not end here; from this capability other elements can also be derived by other branches of government. Thus, generative models are capable of drawing photorealistic images, writing text, and composing music; furthermore, they can create artificial data for the training of other ML models. Concerning the generative models, there is the main stream kind such as Generative Adversarial Network GAN and Variational Auto Encoder VAE. In its implementation it uses two neural networks; one neural network is called the generator and the other neural network is called the discriminator; turns between these two until it reaches the best solution. On the other hand, VAEs learn with the help of two mappings of the input data to the latent space and back to produce new data samples.

One of the core findings of this paper is that deep learning and generative AI are among the most critical advancements in today's applications. The use of variants of ANN, specifically deep learning models, in healthcare, helps in the analysis of medical images to diagnose diseases such as cancer with the same efficiency of professionals. This can be helpful in places where datasets are scarce and medical data cannot be collected from people for research, while the use of generative AI helps to create synthetic data from the existing ones in order to avoid any violation of patient's privacy. In the automotive industry they are used to support perception systems to power self-driving cars, and allow to navigate them. These systems can be trained by generative AI to simulate driving conditions to minimize the extended test drive reality.

In finance areas, the deep learning systems impact huge amount of data to identify the fraudulent transactions and market trends. generative AI shall generate new probable market situations to apply stress testing of the models, so financial models shall be reliable under changed conditions. In entertainment, deep learning improves the recommendation service systems that suggest personalized users' preferences. The advancement in generative AI has embarked on transforming the creation of image, video, music, script writing among others, taken the creation to the next level and automating the entire process.

However, there are notable challenges on the means of applying deep learning and generative AI in embedded systems. It can however be defined as a computer system that is designed for specific control tasks such as controlling heating and cooling system of motor vehicle, radio communication in aircrafts and cars, weather forecast and control, traffic control, telecommunication equipment etc. Embedded system has following characteristics – It normally has a constraint computation capability It has a constraint memory space It requires low power consumption. These limitations require unique procedures for creating a model as well as improving it. In this sense, model pruning, quantization, and knowledge distillation techniques are used to make DL models optimal for the embedded systems. In addition, GPUs, TPUs, and even NPUs that are tailor-made for such hardware are used to boost the performance of these models on smart devices.

The combination of deep learning and generative AI in the embedded systems has the potential of breaking barriers to numerous possibilities. In smart home devices, deep learning models help elements such as voice control, hand movement control, and recommended services for users where the notable factor is the convenience of interacting with smart devices. Generative AI is another type, which can produce synthetic voices or create unique content for a customer, thus giving the customer a better result or experience. In wearable technology, deep learning interprets quantitative data or bio signals to timely inform management of health status and fitness. The kind of intelligence that manifests as generative can run tests to generate all sorts of health conditions and thus assist in the creation of individual wellness programs.

The evolution of the deep learning and generative AI from theories to application has passed through important milestones. Backpropagation developed in the 1980s paved way for training neural networks that are deep. CNNs altered the paradigm of image processing; RNNs and a few of its types, including LSTM, progressed the state and future of natural language understanding. Recognizing the limitations of pre-2015 AI, researchers introduced GANs and VAEs to improve the efficiency of the new content production by adding the ability to generate contents with realism.

The future of deep learning as well as generative AI is expected to advance further in the near future. Neuromorphic computing which aims to replicate the structure of the brain is regarded as one of the development frontiers in AI. Edge AI is also known as the concept that allows bringing new artificial intelligence computational capabilities closer to the source of data and is expected to become the groundbreaker in terms of near real-time applications in use cases of self-driving cars, industrial automation, etc. AI has been shown to integrate with other technologies like blockchain and quantum computing new opportunities which can be explored in different fields are likely to be realized.

Thus, regarding deep learning and generative AI as the next step in innovations, the related ethical issues or paradoxes are yet to be solved. The issue of bias in AI, peoples' data protection, or the inability to explain AI-based decisions is the primary challenges that need to be resolved in order to achieve the proper and non-biased AI utilization. Hence, developing the specific procedures for designing the ethical AI and the implementing the regulations for governing the risks is indispensable for turning the maximum of AI into the positive impact on society.

deep learning and generative AI are the two revolutionism features through which machines can learn from the data feed and create new data patterns. When implemented in the embedded systems, they raise some considerable integration challenges and this defines the innovation process in the different fields. With these advancements, it will demand the proper addressing of the ethical issues and the correct application of these technologies to add value the society. This book would be the single source of information that would help individuals write deep learning and generative AI algorithms on embedded systems and existing platforms and would tie the theoretical part with real-life examples.

1.2 Importance and Applications

Deep learning and generative AI are among the technologies introduced as central frameworks in the contemporary advancements influencing the number of spheres. This dwells on their capacity to perform information processing tasks which include the analysis, interpretation, and generation of information that is precise and innovative in the manner it is processed because of the human factor. These technologies are revolutionizing the face of business and production and are hence highly relevant in societies that are founded on information.

Still, another advantage of deep learning is that this technique has impacted the health sector in a positive way is a proven fact. Examples of application areas include for instance medical imaging, the deep learning algorithm has been utilized in enhancing diagnosis this encompasses identification of tumor, fracture, and other diseases. Currently, radiologists employ these AI systems to supplement diagnosis which has raised early identification ratios and patients' health. Besides imaging, other deep learning models of genomics involve the incorporation of relevant DNA markers that are associated with various diseases in treating patients through the creation of individualized medicine products. However, at the same time, such developments are not only enhancing the quality of patients' treatment but also escalating the rate of innovations in the sphere of medicine.

" Today, people cannot separate deep learning from the automobile business, and this is because of the technology of autonomy in controlling a car's operations. " As is the case with any autonomous car, neural networks are the primary aspect since they enable the object recognition, road navigation, and important decisions making as inferred from the cameras, lidars, radars, and other sensors. Currently, various automaking firms such as Ford Motor, Baidu,

Tesla, and Uber decide on utilizing deep learning's aspects to enhance vehicle autonomy. It will reduce the traffic accident rate, enhance the efficiency of vehicles and transform urban transport, it has been said.

The finance and production sectors or the conventional banking and manufacturing sectors have also not lagged behind when it comes to deep learning and generative AI. Three real-time application areas of deep learning algorithms include possibility to use deep learning algorithms in the fraud detection systems where, for example, several transactions can be analyzed simultaneously and certain patterns that reflect fraud can be defined. This precautionary measure of security helps in protecting the consumers and the institutions from being defrauded their cash. Also, generative AI models are used to model some economic conditions that would be helpful to the traders and analysts in the achieving of their objectives. They are applied to the stress analysis of the financial management strategies since they produce artificial data resembling the real market data.

As regarding the entertainment sector, deep learning and generative AI have numerous and rather distinctive applications. Netflix and Spotify, and etc. are digital platforms that use fast developing artificial intelligence such as deep learning in recommendation systems in delivery of services to its users. Generative AI on the other hand interferes with disruptions in content generation. Synthesizing songs with the assistance of artificial intelligence, scripts for a movie or the play as well as paintings by artificial creations do not appear to be miraculous, therefore, opening up new opportunities and horizons. For instance, OpenAI's GPT-3 recently attracted the attention of many due to the ability to write relatively realistic and contextually appropriate texts, for example, in writing, one can use it with writers, journalists, bloggers or anyone to create content.

While, generative AI and deep learning are two such AI technologies that benefits the retail sector most namely in customer service and inventory. Automation conducted by means of self-service with the assistance of AI-based chatbots, natural language processing answers the questions and complaints. Pricing-based service delivery systems improve the customer's experience since other employees can attend to other important issues. Further, deep learning algorithms help retailers to handle the stock better by observing the pattern of the demand, and thereby reduce the cases of instances where goods such as fresh produce remain in shops and end up going to waste, or those where popular items shift off the shelves faster than the retailer's stock.

Manufacturing is also one of the domains where deep learning and generative AI have big potential to make a difference. Predictive maintenance primarily uses deep learning to identify from sensors installed on the machines when the machinery is likely to breakdown. This means that maintenance is done on time hence minimizing on time lost due to breakdowns and in the long run ensuring that the machinery last long. Generative AI is beneficial in product design because it can search wide space of design solutions and thus create new products and enhance current ones.

Deep learning and generative AI's possibilities include input in the sphere of environmental protection. The proper use of natural resources is also becoming enhanced through the use of AI models. For instance; through the picture recognition, deep learning algorithms can perform the following tasks; detect the rate of deforestation, conserve endangered species, and determine the effects of climate change. Thanks to generative AI, the latter can predict how the environment would be if such or such change occurred and estimate the efficiency of many conservation policies.

Deep learning and generative AI have brought significant changes in education sector and in the way of teaching and learning. Intelligent tutoring systems based on artificial neural network allow integrating the features of student learning activities into the distinct contexts, tailored to the student's abilities. These systems can pinpoint out where students are weak and suggest ways through which students can be helped to strengthen their knowledge. Educational tools like exercises and quizzes can be developed through generative AI based on the learning rate and preferred learning style of the individual student which make education easier and efficient.

Another area of application that has been noted as one of the many uses of generative AI is in drug development. Conventional strategies for reaching new therapies are tedious and costly. Generative AI models can boost this process as the structure and properties of potential drug candidates can be predicted and this will help to identify optimistic compounds faster with less money. This can be potentially dire in terms of putting new products through the market in the pharmaceutical industry enhanced efficiency.

However, when deep learning and generative AI with different applications are reconciled, it has its negative impacts as well. It must also be said that specific aspects, such as, for instance, bias in AI tools and models, as well as the issue of misuse of such systems, are truly ethical in nature. For instance, if bias as well as discrimination exist in the learning data, then AI systems will due to its reinforcement learning model reproduce discriminations and inequality in aspects such as employment, credit, crime and investigation among others. Therefore, the proactive strategy for the AI systems' creation should consider the potential methods to mitigate these threats and restore the public's confidence in AI solutions through transparency and accountability.

Another one is computational intensity of the process, as it is when deep learning methods are used, as these usually require intricate calculations and consumable energy. This is easily explained when dealing with signals as many a time the resource with which one is working with is in some way or the other constrained. Some of the obstacles include the below-mentioned points: A few new technologies in the hardware front like the specific AI chips, edge computing has averted these challenges relating to the deep learning models' deployment in the systems which are lessor in terms of the hardware resources.

perhaps, there can be no more appropriate relevance for deep learning and generative AI today. These technologies are being developed to address so many issues in day-to-day life and virtually every industry starting with health, automobiles, finance and entertainment. Their effectiveness in analyzing - interpreting and even generating data of better accuracy and innovation is already altering our existence. Thus, the issue of the ethical dilemmas of deep learning and generative AI as well as the analysis of what has to be done to eliminate the barriers that may prevent the positive use of AI technologies in future will remain crucial in the future. However, as you would expect with any look into the future there are innumerable possibilities for these technologies and the progression that They will help bring is still out there.

1.3 Challenges in Embedded Environments

Today, embedded systems are nearly ubiquitous, present in smartphones and smart home, machines and equipment of various industries, and self-driving cars. These systems are often defined by the fact that they have a specific purpose within this kind of larger system, and often have real-time requirements and restricted processing capability. Integration of deep learning and generative AI area into embedded environments has positive implications of moving to the next level, but it comes with its own set of issues. Indeed, these challenges stand from basic challenges like the results of the chosen hardware, power consumption, results of the data management, and results of the data security.

Hardware Limitations

Of course, one of the key concerns of embedded environments of any kind is the fact that almost invariably the amount of hardware is limited. Embedded systems also stand apart from the desktop or the cloud computing areas in that those systems are always restricted in the number of resources including the CPU, memory, or storage space. This limitation poses a severe threat to the possibility of applying deep learning models since education of these models usually requires many computations. For example, to train a DNN or carry out a complex generative model normally needs high computation ability and large storage for weights and much more processes' outcomes.

For these constrains, several methods have been invented. Approaches such as pruning, quantization, and knowledge distillation are usually applied to reduce the size and overcome the growth problem of neural networks at the cost of a minimal decline in the results. The first one is about the pruning of neurons or connection that are not expected to enhance the model's performance while the second one decrease the precision of the weights and activations that are used in the neural networks. Knowledge distillation is a mechanism in which knowledge transfer occur from a large and complex model termed as the teacher to a small and less complex model termed as the student. However, even with these techniques, it's still rather a great challenge to achieve the balance between the performance of the model and the resources taken for its training.

Power Efficiency

Power optimization is another constraint of embedded systems that is usually depicted by portable battery-operated devices like smart phones, smart watches, IoT sensors and so on. Almost all DL models including CNNs and RNNs can be computationally and therefore power hungry. But for the computations in the models in the embedded devices, the battery will easily get depleted hence offering very limited time of use and durability of the device.

To make the usage of power more effective, researchers and engineers are also exploring the utilization of the incorporated hardware accelerators that include GPU, TPU, specially designed NPUs and a lot more. These are A I accelerators intended for the computations such as required in neural networks, and they do it at a higher efficiency per watt less than big processors. Besides, largely efficient AI-friendly algorithms as well as new generation power saving technologies like dynamic voltage and frequency scaling (DVFS) are also being developed. Nevertheless, integrating these hardware and software solutions in different kinds of embedded systems is still relatively quite a hard and time-consuming process.

Real-Time Processing

As for the key applications of embedded systems, quite many of them include autonomous driving, robotics, and industrial automation which all need real-time processing. These systems need to analyze data and output responses within very short time frames as always, the emphasis is on safety as well as maximum efficiency. It is difficult to achieve real-time performance with the deep learning models because the training of complex neural networks, by their very nature, requires time.

To deal with real-time measurement issues, model optimization, pipeline parallelism, edge computing came into use. Model optimization is often used to lessen the inference time by modifying the model structure and using proper algorithms. Pipeline parallelism is a process in which the entire processing pipeline is divided into sub-tasks to have multiple of them, which results in a lower overall latency. Edge computing enables computation to be done closer to the source of data, this reduces on the amount of data that needs to be transmitted to centralized server and also less response time. However, there are still some issues that have not been solved sufficiently well in different types of applications of embedded systems where the actions have to be in real-time.

Data Management

These factors indicate that complex variables of an embedded system are usually in a system where data is limited and the bandwidth is constrained.

These are challenging in a way mainly due to the acquisition, sorting and transmission, in weak service zones, of a large amount of information. The challenges often observed here pertain to the procuring of labelled data for the training of deep learning models since, as is known, such models are commonly trained on vast databases.

Among the number of approaches, which are applied to solve the problem of data management, we can mention the following; Federated learning and transfer learning. Federated learning helps in training the models from the device but using the Decentralized data rather than forwarding data to be used in training hence enhancing the privacy. Transfer learning involves using pre-existing normally trained on large datasets and transferring them to new usually small datasets optimized for new tasks. All these approaches can significantly reduce the demands as to the data and improve the quality of model in the data-poor environment.

However, the effective solution to the management of data in the different and often in the dynamically changing embedded systems still remains rather a delicate issue.

Security and Privacy

Security and privacy are always a primary concern in the embedded applications especially when it comes to handling confidential information or in relation to health, finance, and personal electronic gadgets. Cyber threats are frequently directed towards embedded systems since the latter is widely applied in various fields with different protection levels. Security measures regarding deep learning models and data and the limitation of access to unauthorized users are some important issues.

So, techniques like SMPC (secure multi-party computation), HE (homomorphic encryption), DP (differential privacy etc. are being pioneered to improve the security and privacy of the AI models in embedded systems. MPC is the technique that enables two or more parties to evaluate a function over their inputs without revealing those inputs to other parties. HE allows computation on encrypted data while the data is still encrypted, which makes the process secure. Differential privacy introduces noise in the data to hide specific sensitive information while preserving the rest of the data's usefulness. Nevertheless, using these security measures in the resource-constrained embedded environments implies that the overhead of security should be functionally optimized with respect to performance and resource consumption trade space.

Scalability and Flexibility

Jensen and Nielsen show that scaled up and flexibility are two concerns which if deep learning models are to be used in the embedded systems they have to meet. In some cases, such systems may be supposed to change the rates of work, or the gross character of the milieu in which such systems exist, in terms of the special use of the system. As would be expected, it also raises the issue of how deep learning models can become efficient and learn new conditions.

It is worth stating that these challenges are being dealt with in the following manners like the use of the modular and scalable architectures and the use of the adaptive analysis algorithms. As has already been mentioned, the modularity directly connects the relations between the components of the developed model with the opportunity to change these relations if it is necessary, which is why it is also easier to revise and incorporate the system. With regard to particular conditions people require results as close as possible which means that characteristics of the model and the processing scheme may be changed during the work at any time. However, these innovations are not sufficiently developed enough so that, for example, the operating systems interacting with other CE units can be assessed as slightly problematic in relation to achieving simple scalability and flexibility in the infiltrated systems.

Integration and Interoperability

This includes the compatibility of applicable deep learning and Generative AI models with so many installed embedded systems' hardware, software, and data transfer interfaces. Maintenance and integration and compatibilities are rather difficult because of the numerous and various platforms and operating systems and the communication protocols embedded in the devices.

Some of these difficulties, including the creation of AI frameworks and information exchange standards, are being actively discussed and solved at the present stage. Environments such as TensorFlow Lite, ONNX, and Caffe2 are built particularly for deployment purposes in the embedded systems to aid easier conversions. The most common IoT protocols like MQTT, CoAP and OPC-UA are gradually becoming mainstream to guarantee optimal device and systems communication. Nevertheless, the goal of standardizing most of the relevant technologies and of achieving compatibility with different embedded operating environments continues to be a work in progress.

Altogether, the discussed approaches based on deep learning and generative AI face several issues concerning embedded environments, such as limited hardware capabilities as well as power use, real-time computations, and data handling. Responding to these issues calls for improvements on the aspects of the hardware, software, algorithm, and standardization. It can therefore be concluded that the possibilities of deep learning and generative AI in becoming the new ground in embedded systems are as vast as the research and development is unbounded. Thus, the proper and effective implementation of these technologies shall prove vital for their optimization and the further advancement of numerous fields.

CHAPTER 2: FOUNDATIONS OF DEEP LEARNING

2.1 Neural Networks: A Primer

Artificial intelligence which is the present fashion of putting intelligence in computation is grounded on a set of computations called neural networks; these are computations, which mimic the paradigm or design of the human brain. They have changed the approach to learning and machines, have contributed to solving different problems, and are useful in various fields, such as image orientation, language analysis, and auto systems. Here listed is the information the author of this primer wishes to avail in detail overviews of neural networks' concept structure and functionality.

In its simplest definition, a neural network is made up of a series of neurons – artificial neurons or nodes; all the neurons combine to make several layers. Such networks are made to mimic the strategy used by biological neural networks for information processing. In this case, every neuron in a neural network will take inputs, process the inputs, and will also give the outputs. The neurons are organized in a certain design in the form of a network and the junctions between them are termed as synapses, and every synapse has weights that are regulated in the course of training of the particular network to minimize the degree of error of the forecast made. This weighting is one of the most critical processes as far as the training of a neural network is concerned.

One important type of neural network is a perceptron which is, in fact, a neural network with only one layer of neurons or perceptron's. A perceptron can also be regarded as a network node working as follows; It integrates the input features, applies a certain weight to the corresponding feature, and performs a weighted sum at the end of which an activation function is applied to obtain the final output of the perceptron. Therefore, even though perceptron's are relatively useful in the classification of objects into two categories, it can be asserted that they also do not contain the potential for modeling new patterns. To meet this shortcoming, they developed what they refer to as multi-layered structures or feed-forward neural networks. The networks may be more than a combination of the input and output layer neurons, that is the hidden layers to make the network learn other patterns in the given data.

Other parts of the neural network are as follows the activation function which introduces non-linearity into the model. This is actually because if activation functions were not used in networks, the networks would only be useful to produce straight lines – quite restrictive in the kind of problems that they would solve. Some of the activation functions include sigmoid, tanh, and ReLU among others, these are the most frequently used activation functions. which can rescale the input values to the range between 0 and 1 may be useful, especially for binary classification tasks. $Y = 2\tanh(x)/ (1 + \exp(-2x)) - 1$ Thus the tanh scales the input values and gives an output between -1 to 1; hence, gives sufficient freedom to this function than the sigmoid function. The ReLU is also the non-linear activation function in which if the passed input is greater than zero then the ReLU function forwards the input, otherwise, the input is set to zero. This is well beneficial for deep learning essentially because ReLU is immensely easy to implement when building the model.

This is done by calculating the average weight of the links to reduce the fluctuation between the output of the neural network model and the stocks of concern. This is done with a specific method referred to as the backpropagation that determines the partial derivatives of the loss function about all the weights employing elements of calculus. Such gradients are utilized to tweak the weights with the aid of Vanishing or Exploding gradients, the frequently used Stochastic Gradient Descent, or others such as Adam or RMSprop. The given algorithms in simple form try to update the weights of the network in parallel to reduce the loss function to enhance the network performance.

Deep learning can be defined as the neural networks with the many layering known as deep neural networks. Deep networks, in turn, give the possibility of the hierarchic reconstruction of the data and, therefore, some of the connected problems, for example, the recognition of the speech or the image, are solved by the use of deep networks. For instance, in the context of image recognition tasks, the features that exist in the low layers of the deep neural network are straightforward elements of the image – such as edge, contour, and others; while the detectors located in the higher layers of the network are, in fact, more complicated elements of an image such as shapes of the objects present in an image and some cases the objects themselves. Because of the presented hierarchical learning process, the deep structure can learn solutions of state-of-art performance on a great number of tasks.

CNNs can therefore be described as a species in the family of multi-layered Neural Networks useful in tackling data in grid or matrix form such as images. For such processes as the filters or kernel on inputs for identification of edges, and texture among others, the CNNs use the convolutional layers. After the convolutional layers, there are the pooling layers whereby in one way or another, the amount of data is reduced but with a focus on the features. While being quite useful in the identification of images, CNNs are particularly valued for how the hierarchies of spaces are assessed.

The other classes of the neural networks that are employed in the sequential data, the time series data, and the language data are the Recurrent Neural Networks (RNNs). However, unlike the feedforward networks with no-feedback connection mentioned earlier, RNN has a feedback connection that forms a loop and therefore has a memory. It makes it possible for RNNs to identify the existence of the temporal relation of a sequence to predict the inputs of the next sequence. However, standard RNNs have several problems – vanishing and exploding gradients which make it difficult to achieve a satisfactory long-term dependency. That is why, to address such problems, even rather intricate architectures like LSTM networks and GRUs were invented in the first place. Such architectures are; The control mechanisms which are used in the flow of information increase the capability of the networks in learning sequence.

Like any other learning algorithm, there are issues concerning over-training or the extent of fit and generalization for neural networks. Optimization is done in such a way that it fits well to the training data but poorly to the test data, this is known as overfitting. To avoid the problem of overfitting, such methods as dropout, regularization, and data augmentation are used. Dropout as a highly used regularization technique entails stair- or randomly nulling some neurons during training and thus minimizing the dependence of the network on certain features. L1 and L2 regularization which modify the loss function with the root mean square of the weights; thus, avoiding the creation of too complex models. Little more than data augmentation is the procedure of seeking extra samples to train the network by making transformations on the available data to enhance the network's ability to generalize.

neural networks are one of the strongest instruments of machine learning which possesses a high level of flexibility and can model almost any type of relations and solve several tasks. From simple perceptron, basic neural network, deep neural network, CNN to RNN neural networks have advanced in their tasks. Nevertheless, like with any other type of artificial intelligence, there is a set of issues that can be associated with neural networks, such as, for instance, hardware limitations, problems with training, and overfitting. This reason remains an ongoing area of research and development in the instance of neural networks so as more enhancements are made to the field the above challenges are bound the open additional possibilities within the area of AI. It is therefore crucial for anyone who wants to consider the area of AI as a whole to grasp what a neural network is.

2.2 Convolution Neural Networks (CNNs)

Convolutional Neural Networks (CNNs) have emerged as one of the most powerful and widely used architectures in the field of machine learning, particularly for image and spatial data processing. Inspired by the biological visual cortex, CNNs are designed to automatically and adaptively learn spatial hierarchies of features from input images. This makes them exceptionally effective for tasks such as image classification, object detection, and image generation.

At the heart of a CNN is the convolutional layer, which applies a set of filters to the input data. These filters, or kernels, slide over the input image to create feature maps that represent different aspects of the image. For instance, early filters might detect edges or textures, while deeper layers can identify more complex structures like shapes or objects. This hierarchical feature learning is one of the reasons CNNs excel in image recognition tasks.

A fundamental concept in CNNs is the convolution operation itself. The convolution operation involves multiplying each value in the input image by a corresponding value in the filter, summing these products, and then adding a bias term. This process is repeated across the entire image, creating a feature map that highlights the presence of the filter's features. Convolutional layers significantly reduce the number of parameters compared to fully connected layers, which helps in managing computational complexity and preventing overfitting.

Another crucial component of CNNs is the pooling layer, which is used to reduce the spatial dimensions of the feature maps while retaining the most important information. Pooling operations, such as max pooling and average pooling, help in making the network more computationally efficient and robust to variations in input data. Max pooling, for example, selects the maximum value from a group of values within a pooling window, effectively down sampling the feature map while preserving the most significant features.

The architecture of a CNN typically includes multiple convolutional and pooling layers, followed by one or more fully connected layers. The convolutional and pooling layers work together to extract and summarize features from the input image, while the fully connected layers interpret these features to make predictions. The final layer of the network is usually a SoftMax or sigmoid function, which produces probabilities for classification tasks or continuous values for regression tasks.

Training a CNN involves adjusting the weights of the filters and other parameters to minimize the error between the predicted outputs and the actual target values. This process is accomplished through backpropagation and gradient descent. During backpropagation, the gradients of the loss function concerning each weight are computed, and these gradients are used to update the weights via an optimization algorithm such as stochastic gradient descent (SGD) or Adam. Regularization techniques, such as dropout and weight decay, are also employed to prevent overfitting and improve generalization.

One of the key advantages of CNNs is their ability to learn translation-invariant features. Because the filters are applied across the entire image, CNNs can recognize features regardless of their position within the image. This property makes CNNs particularly effective for tasks where spatial hierarchies are important, such as object detection and image segmentation.

Advanced CNN architectures, such as Alex Net, VGGNet, GoogLeNet, and ResNet, have further enhanced the capabilities of CNNs. AlexNet, introduced in 2012, was one of the first deep CNNs to achieve state-of-the-art performance on the ImageNet dataset, demonstrating the effectiveness of deep learning for image classification. VGGNet, known for its simplicity and depth, uses a uniform architecture with small 3x3 convolutional filters and has been influential in the design of subsequent networks. GoogLeNet, with its inception modules, introduced the concept of network-in-network and depth wise separable convolutions, improving computational efficiency. ResNet, or Residual Networks, introduced the idea of residual connections to mitigate the vanishing gradient problem in very deep networks, allowing for the training of extremely deep architectures.

The success of CNNs has extended beyond image processing to other domains. For instance, CNNs have been applied to video analysis, where they can capture spatial and temporal features from sequences of frames. In natural language processing (NLP), CNNs have been used for text classification and sentiment analysis by treating text as a 1D spatial structure. The ability of CNNs to learn hierarchical feature representations has made them versatile and effective across various types of data.

Despite their strengths, CNNs also face certain challenges. One major challenge is the requirement for large amounts of labeled data for training. While data augmentation techniques can help in generating additional training samples, the quality and quantity of data still play a critical role in the performance of CNNs. Another challenge is the high computational cost associated with training deep CNNs, which often necessitates the use of specialized hardware such as GPUs or TPUs.

Moreover, CNNs can be susceptible to adversarial attacks, where small, imperceptible perturbations to the input data can lead to incorrect predictions. Addressing these vulnerabilities is an ongoing area of research, aiming to enhance the robustness and security of CNN models.

To solve some of these issues, scientists are always on the lookout for newer advancements and improvements in CNN architectures and preparing strategies. However, some approaches against the data and computational problems of CNNs are the following Transferred learning where deep models trained for general use are fine-tuned for specific applications, and Efficient architectures like MobileNets and EfficientNets.

Therefore, there is no doubt that CNNs are among the key findings in the present advancement of machine learning and computer vision. Because of the feature that they enable learning and encoding of spatial features in a sequentially advancing manner, they have had immense applicability, not isolated to image recognition. Concerning the successes and further evolution of the CNNs, there is a requirement to address the issue related to the data requirements and computations as well as the model stability issues. As the research and development of this area has advanced, CNNs will be expected to continue to contribute to the development of innovation and development of different industries, and hence promote the continuing development and acclaim of artificial intelligence and AI applications in various sectors.

2.3 Recurrent Neural Networks (RNNs) and Long Short-Term Memory (LSTM)

Recurrent Neural Networks (RNNs) and Long Short-Term Memory (LSTM) networks are essentially particular varieties of neural networks that are developed to work with sequential data. They are primal in operating and prognosis for sequences when the order and context of the data are important such as time series, language understanding, and speech recognition. Those architectures can be examined about their structures and functions, and the improvements LSTM networks introduced to overcome the drawbacks of regular RNNs.

Recurrent Neural Networks (RNNs)

RNNs are designed to recognize patterns in sequences of data by maintaining a form of memory about previous inputs. Unlike feedforward neural networks, which process data in a single pass, RNNs incorporate information from previous time steps through recurrent connections. This means that the output of the network at a given time step depends not only on the current input but also on the previous hidden states, creating a dynamic temporal context.

The basic architecture of an RNN includes an input layer, a hidden layer with recurrent connections, and an output layer. At each time step, the input is processed by the hidden layer, which updates its state based on the current input and the previous hidden state. This updated hidden state is then used to compute the output and is passed to the next time step. Mathematically, the hidden state at the time it is computed Despite their theoretical beauty, basic RNNs have numerous issues, mainly to do with the vanishing and exploding gradient issues. In training, backpropagation through time (BPTT) is employed to update the weights by doing backpropagation through the whole sequence. However, it has been observed that when sequences are long, gradients either die out (vanishing gradient) or become very large (exploding gradient) and hence cannot be learned effectively to train the network.

Long Short-Term Memory (LSTM) Networks

For this purpose, later in 1997, Sepp Hochreiter and Jürgen Schmidhuber proposed a new form of RNN categories called Long Short-Term Memory Networks. LSTMs are a particular type of RNN that has been explicitly developed to model long-term dependencies and therefore address the vanishing gradient problem due to a more complex design of the framework based on memory cells and gating mechanisms.

An LSTM network is composed of several key components:

Memory Cells: These are special units that sustain the state over long periods. LSTMs are a special kind of RNN that permits the network to remember long-term dependencies because they contain memory cells in addition to the regular hidden states of standard RNNs.

Gates: The information content of LSTMs is always regulated by gates in terms of directing data to the memory cells. There are three broad types of gates.

Forget Gate: This gate determines the data that needs to be dumped in the memory cell from the data received by the memory cell. It accepts the previous hidden state as well as the current input and uses a sigmoid function to get the values between [0 and 1] calculated as to how much detail should be neglected.

Input Gate: The output gate samples when new information should be written in the memory cell. It consists of two parts: an activation function deciding which of the weights of the cell should be updated and a hyperbolic tangent function that supplies possible values for updating the cell state.

Output Gate: This gate regulates the information that is to be outputted or transferred out of the memory cell to the other related circuits. Using short-circuit operation, it synthesizes the broken updated memory cell state and current input to get the final output.

The LSTM architecture provides several advantages over traditional RNNs:

Mitigation of Vanishing Gradient Problem: This is well facilitated by the gating mechanisms and memory cells of the LSTMs which enables the maintenance of gradients while back-propagating to help the network in the learning of long-term dependencies.

Improved Long-Term Dependency Learning: LSTMs can keep patterns in memory cells, and as such, can learn and remember sequences over long periods and so are good at tasks with long-term dependencies such as language modeling and machine translation.

Enhanced Stability: LSTMs are relatively less sensitive to the arising of the exploding gradient problem because of the employing of gating mechanisms to control the channel of gradients and updates.

Applications of LSTM Networks

LSTM networks have been successfully applied to a wide range of applications:

Natural Language Processing (NLP): LSTMs are applied in most NLP tasks and include sentiment analysis, language modeling, machine translation, and text generation. They are useful in the case of variable-length sequences of text and when the model needs to capture contextual information.

Speech Recognition: In general, in the case of speech recognition systems, LSTMs will be beneficial in learning the temporal characteristics of the audio and enhancing the transcription.

Time Series Forecasting: They are applied in predicting the financial future, weather prediction, and any field that involves sequential data. The degree of dependency is long-standing, making them reliable for predicting current trends based on their historical background.

Challenges and Future Directions

However, there are some disadvantages in the use of LSTMs as presented herein below. They can be especially intricate, and frequently, the determination of the model's solution at the intersection considerably depends on the choice of hyperparameters. However, it is important to note that despite this, LSTMs do no way steer clear of all the issues due to the inherent nature of such development, for example, the issues of complexity or interpretability of the developed models.

Other advancements made in sequence modeling have been brought into revelation by the introduction of other architectures such as the Gated Recurrent Units (GRUs) and the Transformer models. Thus, LSTMs and GRUs have the same predictiveness, but the latter does not request as much computation time because the separate forget and input gates are absent and are included in the update gate instead. The transformer models assumed by Vaswani et al. in 2017 apply an attention mechanism to operate on sequence where recurrent connections are not present, hence, enabling more tasks to be performed in parallel as well as more efficiently.

RNNs together with LSTM networks are stated to be actual progress in an approach to the management of sequential attributes. There were the original RNNs that were introduced before and their purpose was to model the temporal dependencies for which they however had certain problems the handling of which was extended by LSTMs that enhanced the learning of long dependency. Thus, they are useful and applied in such areas as NLP, speech recognition, and prediction of time series data. Further studies will still be carried out in sequence modeling and as architectures and techniques grow and expand, more improvements to the capacity of sequence modeling will still be discovered with potential in different applications available.

2.4 Advanced Architectures: Transformers, GANs, and Autoencoders

As a result of the ever-changing new inventions that are being imposed in artificial intelligence, new architectures include transformers, GANs, and autoencoders, which are promising technologies. Thus, familiarity with these architectures is crucial for best using and, maybe, extending their potential in different fields.

Transformers

Transformers, which are discussed in the paper by Vaswani et al. from 2017, have become a game-changer in NLP and other research areas. Unlike recurrent neural networks (RNNs), and convolutional neural networks (CNNs), the Transformers make use of a self-attention mechanism which helps the model to work on sequences of data more efficiently.

The main departure of Transformers is the 'self-attention,' which enables the model to prioritize some parts of the input sequence over others. This mechanism allows the model to spot the relations between the words or tokens, and this is irrespective of the position of the token. The self-attention mechanism is implemented through several key components: The self-attention mechanism is implemented through several key components:

Attention Scores: Attention scores are calculated for each token in the sequence to know how much attention has to be paid to the other tokens. This is done using three vectors: queries, keys, and values which are the tokens of input data. The attention scores are obtained by multiplying the query vector with the key vector and then passing through the softmax function on the integration of the array.

Multi-Head Attention: To understand several kinds of interactions and dependencies Transformers use several heads of attention. Every head performs self-attention independently, and after this, all the outputs that have been produced by working with different heads are transformed using one more linear layer. This makes it possible for the model to assume characteristics of the input sequence in one or different aspects.

Positional Encoding: Transformers do not know the concept of positional order of the sequences so positional encodings are incorporated in the input embeddings to pass the sequence number. This encoding is useful in as much as it assists the model in being able to identify between different positions and ordering of the sequence.

Transformers are the current state-of-the-art models in different NLP tasks such as machine translation, text generation, and question answering. Some popular transformer-based models are BERT, GPT, and T5 models respectively referring to Bidirectional Encoder Representations from Transformers, Generative Pre-trained Transformers, and Text-to-Text Transfer Transformers. Such models have shown excellent performance in both comprehension and synthesis of human language and as such have made great advances in language-oriented programs.

Generative Adversarial Networks (GANs)

GANs or the subject of the current paper came into existence in the year 2014 by the work of Ian Goodfellow and his co-authors. GANs are made up of two neural networks – the generator network and the discriminator network, which are arch rivals. The generator creates the synthetic data samples in turn the discriminator decides on the credibility of the samples created by the generator as real or fake.

The training process at each iteration is done through playing a two-player game First player known as the generator plays the data samples and tries to build data samples that look like real data Second player known as the discriminator tries to classify the data samples correctly. This adversarial process drives both networks to improve their performance iteratively: This competition process also forces the two networks to optimize this process continually:

Generator: The generator uses random noise as input and gives out synthetic data samples as output. It aims to produce samples that are as close to the original data as possible, thus 'deceiving' the discriminator into thinking that the samples are real.

Discriminator: The discriminator takes as input nodes real data samples and generated data samples and the purpose of this node is to classify the input data into either real or forged. It aims to affirm whether the presented samples are 'authentic' or 'fake' – evidence that would be extremely valuable for the generator in improving the production of such fakes.

If further, the loss functions of the generator and the discriminator have been chosen to define the objectives and roles of both networks. The disappearance of the generator is calculated on the premise of the error of the discriminator so that the generator can design more hyper-realistic samples of the required data. On the other hand, the loss of the discriminator depends on the ability of the discriminator to distinguish between the real sample and the generated samples.

They have procured quite good results in various tasks like image synthesis, stylization, and augmentation. Among those tasks, it has been used for high-quality image synthesis, realistic painting, and enlargement of the data set for the training of artificial neural networks. Nevertheless, GANs are not without problems: For instance, sample generation which has been skewed to the different modes, where the generator has carved out samples with only small variation; training instability whereby the adversarial process can lean.

Autoencoders

Autoencoder is a deep learning model or a neural network used to solve unsupervised learning problems, more often used to carry out data compression and representation. Autoencoder: The base aim of the autoencoder is to compress and reconstruct the input data reducing the reconstruction error to the maximum extent. An autoencoder consists of two main components:

Encoder: It marks the time at which the various themes first reference or the lowering, in terms of dimensionality, of the data input or the transformation of the input data into the lower dimensionality space. It compacts the data and it does so with the help of learning the main characteristics of the offered input set. In most of cases, the encoder is made out of one or more layers of neural networks responsible for the initial dimensionality reduction of the input signal.

Decoder: The Decoder reverses the values from the reciprocal representation in the positioning of the latent space representation. It tries to undo all that the encoder has done to provide the closer approximation of the data as possible. It also includes one or fully connected multi-layer neural network layer which lowers or raises the dimensions of the latent representation back to the initial dimensions.

Its training objective is therefore to reduce a measure of the reconstruction loss or the degree of distortion in the data that flows through that autoencoder. Some examples of choices of losses are mean squared error for the regression of the kind of data, and the binary cross entropy for the binominal type of data.

Autoencoders have various applications, including: There are several types of autoencoders and the uses include:

Dimensionality Reduction: Some of what autoencoders can do are similar to higher-dimensional data dimensionality reduction techniques such as the Principal Component Analysis (PCA) but the application is more flexible and possibly non-linear.

Data Denoising: Denoising autoencoders are learned on noisy input and it is utilized in the processes of image denoising and other related tasks.

Anomaly Detection: There is how autoencoders are of use in identifying unusual data points by measuring the reconstruction error that depicts data outliers.

Autoencoder networks have their enhanced forms: Variational Autoencoder (VAE) that involves probabilistic interpretation of the latent space to make it capable of generating samples and performing more comprehensive tasks. VAEs capture an embedding distribution over latent space, thus VAEs can sample from a diverse range of coherent samples in a natural manner.

Special architectures like Transformers, GANs, and Autoencoders have made great milestones in the domain of machine learning and artificial intelligence. Transformers have become the new generation models in NLP providing self-attention and easy scalability. The use of GANs has provided a novel method of following a data generation and augmentation process due to the adversarial training method it uses. Due to autoencoders, it has become possible to compress the data, de-noise it, and even learn its representation. All of these architectures resolve certain issues and create new opportunities for using such applications in spheres that require AI and contribute to the further development of this area. **2.5 Training Deep Learning Models**

Deep learning training is a process that has several steps, hence it is slightly complicated but highly rewarding when done appropriately depending on the type of model to be used, data selection and processing, as well as the model testing, and tuning. The present guide is designed to give a brief description of the general training process, concerning the definitions of the main ideas and referencing examples where necessary.

1. Data Preparation

In training any deep learning model, the most important and first stage which is data preprocessing is paramount. You need good and clean data for training models to enhance the quality of your model. Some of the tasks that come under data preparation include data gathering, data cleansing, data enhancement, and data partitioning.

Data Collection: Data that are related to the problem to be solved should be accumulated. For instance, if you are working on a model that is to be trained for an image classification task, you may obtain thousands of images, which are tagged.

Data Cleaning: Make sure that these results are free from any form of errors or any form of inconsistency. This might entail situations where there were duplicate records of the same sample, some samples, and values that were missed out and wrongly identified samples.

Data Augmentation: Increase the amount of training data and use the methods of data augmentation like rotation, scaling, and flipping in images. Data augmentation is useful to make the model better to generalize since it increases the amount of different input data. For example, if you are using cat images, it is possible to add to the dataset, rotated or cropped images of cats.

Data Splitting: For evaluation of the algorithm, split the collected data into training data sets, cross-validation data sets, and test data sets. The training set is used to update the parameters of the model, the validation set is used to select the hyperparameters, and the model is tested on the test data to measure the accuracy of the model on unseen data. A possible division for this is for 70% for training, 15% for the validation, and the remaining 15% for the testing.

2. Model Selection

The architecture of the deep learning model depends on the type you are selecting to use and properly selecting this architecture can make a very big difference in your model's effectiveness. The selection depends on the type of problem one is trying to solve and the kind of data available for analysis.

Convolutional Neural Networks (CNNs): Ideal for image-related tasks. For example, Mnist's written digits data set can be classified by using any particular CNN like ResNet or VGGNet.

Recurrent Neural Networks (RNNs): Suitable for sequential data the analyses of which require ordering, for instance, time series or text. The implementation of the RNN or its improvement, known as LSTM, can be used for forecasting stock prices in consideration of records.

Transformers: Can be useful when it comes to natural language processing. For example, you could use Transformer models such as BERT or GPT to classify certain movie reviews as positive or negative.

Autoencoders: As it is effective in cases where no guidance is given on how specific features of the data relate to one another, it is valuable for instance in data clustering or removing noise. An autoencoder is useful for tasks such as denoising of images or simply dimensionality reduction for visualization purposes.

3. Model Training

The training of deep learning models involves; feeding the training data into the model, computing the loss, and updating the weights on the model using optimization algorithms. Key steps include:

Forward Propagation: Once again feed the input data through the network to have the output predictions. For example, in a CNN for image classification forward propagation entails going through an image to convolution and pool layers to arrive at the class probabilities.

Loss Calculation: Derive "loss', ' the difference between the data generated by the predicted model and the true label. The loss functions are plain and are the following: the softmax cross entropy loss used in classifying models and the mean squared loss in regression models. For instance, let there be an inclination whose probability has been established to be, say, 0. 7 for a cat image when it is a cat the cross entropy will be least which is a good indication that our prediction is as required.

Backpropagation: If needed compute or differentiate the values used for updating the weights through the chain rule of calculus for the loss of the model of the weights. These gradients tell in which direction and by how much the weights have to be updated to reduce the loss.

Optimization: Perform the weights update in the model using the form of an optimization algorithm. Among them, there is Stochastic Gradient Descent (SGD) and two more, Adam and RMSprop. For instance, Adam has a different learning rate for weights will enhance the convergence rate than SGD.

4. Hyperparameter Tuning

The other is the set of parameters referred to as hyperparameters which do not change with the training of the model, but are significant determinants of the model's training process. They include; the learning rate, batch size, the number of layers, and the number of units in each of the layers. Hyperparameters optimization means the fine-tuning of those parameters that provide the best performance of the model.

Scientifically search hyperparameters at various rat orders, the process of which is computational. Thus, one would have learned rates, that are 0. 001, 0. 01, 0. 1, and batch sizes 32, 64, and 128 to check the outcome with the best combination.

Take hyperparameters randomly with a given range. This method is often more efficient than grid search, this is more evident when dealing with high hyperparameter dimensions.

Have to employ the methods with probabilities to find the optimal hyperparameters. This strategy involves creating a surrogate model of the objective function so that it can be used in selecting the best hyperparameter values.

5. Model Evaluation

However, it is now necessary to evaluate the performance of the model on the test set to ensure that it can generalize to unseen data.

When dealing with classification problems, assess the percentage of right classifying of instances. For instance, a model that can classify ninety of one hundred test images correctly then the model will be described as having ninety percent accuracy.

Metrics of this type provide other information regarding how effective the model is and prove especially important when the data set is skewed. Specificity always gives the ratio of true positives to false positives while sensitivity gives the ratio of true positives to the total actual positives. F1 score is described as a measure that is derived by taking the harmonic mean of two values, namely precision and recall.

The confusion matrix provides the total, right, and wrong values and thereby also helps to determine at what stage the model is going wrong.

6. Model Deployment

When a model has been developed and tested this can be applied in solving real-life problems Thus, the meanings of the model used in this context are concerned as they are relevant to use in practical use. This encompasses replacing the model with a production environment in an attempt to translate it into new data.

Employ a serving platform to serve the requests and the predictions given out by the model. Prominent examples of such solutions are TensorFlow Serving and NVIDIA Triton.

It is also important to check periodically how the model works in production to notice drifting trends out of the observed range. It is achieved by observing the accuracy and handling the shift in the concept, which is a change in data distribution and the model learning as required.

Example: Training a CNN for Image Classification

Well, let me now assume that you have your data set of images and you wish to train the CNN that is concerned with the classification of cats and dogs. Here's a step-by-step overview of the process: As to the process leading to the aforementioned process, the following holds:

 Collect a cats and dogs dataset. Split the data into a training data set, data validation set, and test data set. In the training set to name but a few the following transformations were used for instance rotation of the images and flipping of the images among others to make the amount of data being fed to the network higher.

 Depending on the expected result of the training, one at some point has to work with VGG16 or ResNet50 CNN architecture. These architectures are built on larger receptive databases and can be fine-tuned for this between cat and dog classification.

Create the CNN model that should have the convolutional layer, the pooling layer as well as the fully connected layer. It can, however, be trained using binary cross entropy loss function and Adam optimizer. The training dataset concerns the model selection and its parameter optimization, and the validation dataset will concern the selection of the right hyperparameters for the modeling.

You should perform a large number of searches regarding the learning rate, size of the batches, and even the number of epochs that you are going to employ. On other occasions, one can settle for either a grid search or a random search to arrive at the appropriate hyperparameters to use.

The majority of it should be directed to the testing phase in other to determine the strength of the model that can be argued as accuracy, precision, recall, and confusion matrix among others. Ensure that the model gets above-par results with the new images even though the model has not encountered the images before.

Design a platform where other people or a specific group of people can submit their images to be uploaded and categorized based on the pre-trained CNN model. This means only one thing: when using it in the operating processes of the company, one has to measure the results, and after some time of getting less than the maximum result – it has to be fine-tuned again to achieve a much higher level of people's response.

The steps that are employed in the creation of deep models are as follows; data pre-processing, model selection, training of the model, optimization of the model, validation of the model and lastly deploying of the model. All these are important in developing models with a high capacity for solving problems since the extent achieved in each step shall define the extent of the whole result. The following are the actual splits and actual usage of the datasets when employed will result in good performance of deep learning models and consequently solve the actual problem. To justify their 'advance,' you should be able to realize them as you construct high-value solutions in the future, assuming that the field will expand in the future as it has in the past.

2.6 Evaluation Metrics and Techniques

It is therefore important and standard practice to assess how well performance deep learning models generalize on unseen data. Measures of performance and method allow us to assess the quality of our model, or its resilience in the face of certain conditions, as well as the practical applicability of the model in certain scenarios. This guide provides information on some of the main evaluation measures and methods used in deep learning together with information on the role of each of them and the types of models that should be evaluated using each of them.

1. Classification Metrics

For classification tasks, where the goal is to assign input data to predefined categories, several metrics are used to measure performance. These metrics provide different perspectives on how well a model is performing and help in understanding its strengths and weaknesses.

Accuracy is the most straightforward metric, representing the proportion of correctly classified instances out of the total instances. It is calculated as

$$\text{Accuracy} = \frac{\text{Number of Correct Predictions}}{\text{Total Number of Predictions}}$$

While accuracy is useful for balanced datasets, it can be misleading in cases of class imbalance, where some classes are underrepresented.

The F1 score combines precision and recall into a single metric by calculating their harmonic mean. It is defined as

$$\text{F1 Score} = 2 \times \frac{\text{Precision} \times \text{Recall}}{\text{Precision} + \text{Recall}}$$

F1 Score. The F1 score is particularly useful when the balance between precision and recall is important.

A confusion matrix provides a detailed breakdown of the model's performance by showing the number of true positives, true negatives, false positives, and false negatives. It helps in understanding which classes are being misclassified and the types of errors being made.

2. Regression Metrics

Mean Squared Error (MSE): MSE measures the average of the squared differences between predicted and actual values. It is calculated as

$$MSE = 1n\sum i$$

$$= 1n(Predicted i - Actual i)2\text{MSE}$$

$$= \backslash frac\{1\}\{n\}$$

$$\backslash sum_{\{i=1\}}^{\{n\}(\backslash text\{Predicted\}_i - \backslash text\{Actual\}_i)^{2MSE}} = n1\sum i$$

$$= 1n(Predicted i - Actual i)2.$$

MSE penalizes larger errors more than smaller ones, making it sensitive to outliers.

Root Mean Squared Error (RMSE): RMSE is the square root of MSE, providing an error metric in the same units as the target variable. It is calculated as RMSE=MSE\text{RMSE} = \sqrt{\text{MSE}}RMSE=MSE. RMSE is useful for understanding the magnitude of prediction errors and comparing models.

R-squared (Coefficient of Determination): R-squared measures the proportion of variance in the target variable that is explained by the model. It is calculated as

$$R2 = 1 - SSresSStotR^2$$

$$= 1$$

$$- \backslash frac\{\backslash text\{SS\}_{\backslash text\{res\}}\}\{\backslash text\{SS\}_{\backslash text\{tot\}}\}R2$$

$$= 1$$

$$- SStotSSres, where\ SSres$$

$\backslash text\{SS\}_{\backslash text\{res\}SSres}$ is the residual sum of squares and SStot

$\backslash text\{SS\}_{\backslash text\{tot\}S}$

Stot is the total sum of squares. R-squared indicates how well the model fits the data.

3. Model Robustness and Generalization

The ability of the model to perform on new data is another aspect as that defines the model's usability. Several techniques and metrics are employed to assess model robustness and generalization: To test model robustness or generalization, several techniques as well as metrics are used as discussed below:

In cross-validation it is done in such a way that the data is divided into several subsets known as the folds and out of these subsets the model is trained on some folds and tested with other folds. This technique has helped in an assessment of the model concerning various facets of the provided data and the effectiveness of the model when tested on the new data is more enhanced. Some of the most familiar kinds of cross-validations include the k-fold cross-validation and the leave-one-out cross-validation among others.

Unlike hold-out validation, the data is firstly split into two differently used sets – training and test data. Meanwhile, the test set is used to test the result of the model and the training set is used to train the model. This approach provides a glimpse of the performance of the model when it is used on unknown data but it is highly dependent on the size of the test dataset.

The learning curves can be such things as the accuracy or the loss of the model as the function of the size of the training data or the number of epochs that were used during the training. They help in understanding the trend of the model in learning from data and differentiate overlearning or underlearning from the data.

4. Model Comparison and Selection

When comparing different models or architectures, it is important to use metrics and techniques that provide a comprehensive view of their performance: When comparing the results of different models or architectures it is necessary to select the metrics and methods that would help to explain advantages and disadvantages of each one:

Other comparative measures that may be used are accuracy, precision, recall, F1, MAE, RMSE, and MSE these may be depending on validation or test. Make sure also that the metrics match the goal and the need of the task that needs to be accomplished.

Should there be significant differences dependent on the means of models then it is recommended to carry out the paired t-tests or the Wilcoxon signed-rank tests. They are enormously useful in determining whether observed differences are real or due to random chance or worsening/improvement.

It also encompasses the ability to recognize that models are of low complexity and possess a high measure of interpretability. Such explicit notation is smarter or possesses better or higher performance in comparison with simple models, but those models are as easy to interpret and analyze as simple models are and they are computationally more expensive. The complicated models might be a little bit confusing and hard to apply in some instances; therefore, it is better to apply relatively simple models in given conditions.

5. Practical Examples

To illustrate the application of these evaluation metrics and techniques, consider two practical examples: an image classification task I am talking of an image classification task and a regression task whereby images of a certain theme could be rated on a scale of 1-10 based on the clarity of the theme depicted.

For instance, get it for case, you are training a CNN to classify images of animals and their classes as cat, dog, and bird. If you were to train the model, we then test the accuracy, precision, recall, and F1 measure it. It would be useful in terms of which classes are being confused with one another and should ideally produce a confusion matrix. Other procedures may be applied with the aim of assessing the effectiveness of the model The effectiveness of the given model may have been tested using the cross-validation method to check how well the model will perform in different tests on the given data set.

For example, when one is developing a model to use to estimate the price for the houses based on the size, location, and the number of rooms. For the degree of accuracy in the machine's predictions they would use metrics such as the MAE, the MSE, and the RMSE. To analyze how much of the variation in house prices the model is explaining we use R-squared. Trends might be helpful in understanding if a model fits given data too well or poorly, that is, up to the point of meeting the necessary condition.

It becomes necessary to assess performance, and generalizability of deep learning models and use some of the evaluation metrics and techniques. To have a full view of the performance of your models, you may also use accuracy, precision, recall, MAE, MSE, R-squared and cross-validation, hold out-validation. This understanding helps in decision-making in the choice, optimization, and deployment models to ensure that they are competent in solving real-world problems.

CHAPTER 3: INTRODUCTION TO GENERATIVE AI

3.1 What is Generative AI?

The latest form of artificial intelligence is generative AI which is also referred to as the shift in paradigm of machine learning and artificial intelligence. In contrast with more or less established forms that AI has been modeled in the sense of pattern recognition or decision-making, generative AI models are capable of generating new data in machine vision, text, audio, or other forms of digital content. The capability for creating content on demand in this manner has far-reaching consequences on relative industries making it possible to fame innovative concepts and ethical concerns in many fields, including artistic and the medical field.

1. The Core Concept of Generative AI

In its crudest sense, generative AI can be defined as models of machine learning that can create new data that was not produced before. These models learn about the system find out the characteristics of a given data set and produce fresh results related to it. It is another approach on large datasets where the model will work with the probability density of the data and then generate new data samples.

For example, the generative AI that has been trained using a data set that corresponds to the actual human images will generate fully realistic images of faces that have not been seen in the real world. Similarly, a corpus-based model can write coherent semantically related, and contextually relevant sentences, paragraphs, or even articles on its own.

2. Key Techniques in Generative AI

In generative AI there are various methods and approaches, which are all effective in their way. The most important examples of such models are Generative Adversarial Networks (GANs), Variational Autoencoders (VAEs), and Transformer-based models.

Generative Adversarial Networks (GANs): Of the generative AI models, those called GANs, which were presented by Ian Goodfellow and his collaborators in 2014, are still in demand. A GAN consists of two neural networks: that is, a generator and a discriminator, these two are used in the Generative Adversarial Network. The generator produces data similar to the actual data, nonetheless, the data arising from this generator is unreal data, on the other side, the discriminator identifies the authenticity of the data. The two networks are trained simultaneously in the following manner which is similar to a game in which the generator is supposed to fool the discriminator while on the other hand, the discriminator's task is to capture fake samples generated by the generator. In the long run, such an approach leads to the production of very credible data bearing in mind that the participants in the case constitute an antagonistic type of relationship.

Variational Autoencoders (VAEs): VAEs are another generative model that differs from GANs in their approach but are also quite potent. VAEs take in the input data and then map it to a significantly lower number of dimensions, and then the network learns to map it back to the original space. In the process, it acquires a probability distribution over the reconstructed latent space by which the model generates new data. This makes VAEs especially useful for applications in which the generated data have to be rich and diverse, but still semantically consistent which might be useful for image generation or anomaly detection.

Transformer-based Models: Transformer models such as GPT (Generative Pre-trained Transformer) by OpenAI in recent years have upended generative AI, especially in natural language processing (NLP). Transformers incorporate self-attention mechanisms, making them products for modeling long-miss dependencies in data and producing coherent rather as pertains to the context. From these models, one can generate essays, answer questions, develop dialogues, as well as write poetry – out-competing existing mechanized models.

3. Applications of Generative AI

To exemplify, generative AI can be applied in various sectors and areas of operation and has a broad and rich use in various settings. Some of the most prominent applications include: Here are some of the most popular areas of its use:

Another area of application of generative AI is in creating new works in art, music, design, etc.; artists leverage generative models to create pieces, say in art, fashion designs, or architectural blueprints that cannot be done ordinarily. For example, there exists the GANs that provide realistic images in portraits, while the Transformers in music or poetry.

In the current world, generative AI is used in the media and entertainment production sectors for tasks such as; writing news articles, and blogs and generating video games and virtual worlds. That not only increases the level of the content production frequency but also allows the creation of content that could be preferred by the particular person.

In healthcare, generative AI applies in the discovery of new drugs, Imaging, and personal health care. For example, both VAEs and GAN are used in the synthesis of new molecules that could be potential drug candidates, AI models create synthetic medical images to enlarge the training dataset towards the further improvement of diagnostic models' performance.

Still, another application of generative AI is to genetically generate more data, synthetic data to add to the database. It is particularly useful when data are scarce if the data available would not be fairly distributed, as is the case for health sciences if there are screwy records, or if fraud is suspected. An important aspect is, in turn, the fact that generative models can also create more training data that can be further used by other models for improvement and simplification of their training.

Some of the current conversational AI and chatbot pioneers are the recent transformer-based generative models such as GPT-3. Such models are in use in customer service platforms, digital voices, and, to an extent, in some of the narrative features.

4. Ethical and Social Implications

The opportunity of generative AI is great, but it comes with several ethical and social issues. It became clear that, on one hand, these models can create photorealistic synthetic media, which is great for entertainment or learning, in a negative way they present threats, including deepfakes, manipulation of content, privacy breaches, and identity theft. The examples of deepfakes where with the help of GANs videos or images of a person talking or acting in a certain way are produced when in fact the person has never done so raises concerns as to the ethical use of artificial intelligence.

However, the use of generative AI as a tool for writing has many more problems, such as authorship and the ownership of the created content. Since creating music or artwork, does the model own the rights to that particular creation? Other applications are the employment of AI-generated content in other sectors such as journalism raises issues of employment loss and the quality of materials that are being produced.

As a result of these problems, there is a shift towards formulation of the rules and standards of ethical Generation AI. Academic scholars and policymakers are developing frameworks to present generative AI as a utopia that brings values of innovation at a similar parity with concern for social values.

5. The Future of Generative AI

This is in a nutshell what generative AI presents for the future: it is very positive and yet very ambiguous. Thus, as models progress in terms of their competencies of generating accurate and valuable results, a broad variety of applications in all domains can be expected. For instance, within the learning domain, the use of generative AI can be targeted at designing a learning environment that can be aligned with the user ID; in the entertainment area, it can mean the creation of an environment produced by AI and resembling a real-world environment – virtual reality.

In return, the time-tested ethical and social problems will have to be addressed and solved appropriately. With the new trends such as generative AI the ideas of transparency, fairness, and accountability for creating AI will be of great value.

 To put it in a nutshell, generative AI is notably more developed than its counterparts in the previous epochs; Moreover, it has the potential to become a significant game changer in the further rise of new industries determining the ways of content generation and consumption in the digital milieu. Still, the actualization of this potential will mean moving through very ethical dangers and ensuring that the technology is applied correctly. In addition to broadening the experiments with generative AI, it is possible to raise the topic of AI and society again, as well as to resume the discussion with leaders all over the world.

3.2 Types of Generative Models

Generation models are a subset, of machine learning models that allow a model to build new examples like the training examples. generative models can generate new data which discriminative models cannot; therefore, they can be used in several applications including image translation, text synthesis, and data enlargement. Here I will describe the most widespread types of generative models and the way they build the data generation processes.

1. Generative Adversarial Networks (GANs)

Generative Adversarial Networks (GANs) are one of the few basic types of generative models and are widely known and used. Proposed by Ian Goodfellow et al., in 2014 GANs are two neural networks known as the generator and the discriminator that are trained in a 'battle'.

The generator's position is to generate synthetic data that looks like the actual one. The system is designed to accept random noise and convert it to an example from the synthetic data distribution.

The discriminator's objective is to evaluate which of the inputs, real or fake, were produced by the generator. It provides a probability that an instance — an image, for example — is real or fake.

During training, the generator and discriminator are locked in a game: the generator attempts to provide the discriminator with fake data in an attempt to make the data as real as possible while on the other hand, the discriminator becomes more sophisticated in identifying the real data from the fake one. In the long run, this adversarial process results in the generation of almost 'real' data by the generator. GANs have been applied in image and video generation, not limited to and including audio and art generation.

Variants of GANs:

Such models produce data that depend on certain input parameters, which means that each next generation is more controlled (generating images of certain objects or styles).

Can be used for style transfer, for example, to transform a photograph to a painting where source and target images are not necessarily mapped.

The resilience of the fundamental GAN is improved by recent enhancements such as better control over the style and features of the images generated particularly used in face generation.

2. Variational Autoencoders (VAEs)

Another wonderful class of generative models with a rich theoretical basis and using concepts of autoencoders in combination with probabilistic methods is Variational Autoencoders or VAEs. It should be recalled that VAEs are designed to capture distribution over the data and, therefore, they can be used to generate new examples.

The Encoder network reconstructs the input data in latent dimension which is pre-defined and constrained equal or below 'd', and every point in the space represents probably distribution which is usually Gaussian.

The decoder network allows the reconstruction of the data from the given latent space representation. Using the present code, the decoder can then sample from this latent space They are then able to generate new instances of data.

VAEs are particularly appropriate in cases where generated data should be stochastic, but continuous, for example in image data, detection of outliers, or generation of additional training data. Thus, one of the major strengths of VAEs relative to other generative models can be noted: while learning the complex distribution of the data, VAEs generate smooth pseudo-realistic variations of the data.

3. Autoregressive Models

Autoregressive models are generative models that generate data in which the current generated data will depend on the previous data that have been generated. These models are by far the most efficient when working with sequential data which can be for instance; Text, Audio, or time series data. These models belong to the category of autoregressive models applied to the image generation field. Both PixelRNN and PixelCNN are sequentially generated and the generation of the image is one pixel at a time in which the probability of any pixel depends on the previously generated pixel. Naturally, this approach is incapable of creating imagery with a very high degree of elaboration.

WaveNet is a new method of synthesizing the raw audio waveform that was introduced by DeepMind, and it uses the autoregressive neural network. It has a voice like a person speaking and has been employed in an application that translates, text to speech.

In the same way that in the natural language processing the autoregressive models like the GPT generate text in an incremental manner word by word such that a current word is dependent on the sequence that was generated. Just as the name suggests GPT models have been used for a variety of tasks such as text completion, translation, and conversational agents.

It is a type of flexible model specifically built for problems where there is a clear temporal or sequential dependency in the given data and as such it has some good applications in language modeling, speech, and time series.

4. Flow-Based Models

Flow-based models are a type of generative model that explicitly learns how to map the data space to latent space and vice versa.

They are used to map a relatively basic distribution, say Gaussian distribution and transform the data distribution by a sequence of operations that are invertible. By performing these transformations one on top of the other, flow-based models can learn generative models of extreme flexibility and expressiveness.

RealNVP is a particular kind of flow-based model, which means that it is straightforward to do exact sampling and density estimation. It is employed in tasks that require high-quality generation besides the ability to estimate the likelihood in a manner that is computationally efficient as in image and audio generation.

Flow-based models are beneficial in a way that they give exact and computationally efficient probability densities so that they are useful when the likelihood of the data is relevant besides the generation of new ones.

5. Diffusion Models

Generative models can also be classified according to the time they were developed, and thus give rise to the more modern diffusion models. They generate data with the diffusion process from the stochastic noise with the use of learned probabilistic models in turn.

It is an approach that is derived from noise generation models with random quantities and gradually enhances the structure of the training data while reducing the noise. Each stage of the diffusion procedure reduces the noise, relative to the possibilities of the neural network that would be required to reverse the diffusion process.

Like DDPMs, these models synthesize data iteratively, gradually modifying random noise in some fashion. They learn how to choose the score that will be utilized in the process of generating the new data with a certain gradient of the data probability distribution.

Such techniques have been used to produce static sample images of very high quality, and the extent of change in these images can be consciously controlled and that is why diffusion models are highly developed and a very active field of research in numerous applied disciplines.

6. Energy-Based Models (EBMs)

Energy-based models are a category of generative models where the probability distribution of the model is determined by an energy function. The energy function 'penalizes' data points that are similar to the training data and 'rewards' data points that are dissimilar.

These are probably one of the oldest classes of EBMs because the energy function is defined over the topology of binary neurons. Such a simplified version is the Restricted Boltzmann Machines (RBMs) which was applied to collaborative filtering and for feature learning.

These models generalize the notion of EBMs to deep neural networks to be able to model high dimensional distribution.

EBMs are more general purpose and can be used for generation as well as classification. Still, training of the EBMs can be a problem because the energy function can be hard to normalize, though contrastive divergence was introduced as an attempt to solve this problem.

Generative models are an effective and rather versatile subgroup of machine learning models that are aimed at producing coherent samples of data in a particular field. Starting from the generative adversarial network GANs up to the variational autoencoder VAEs and until the autoregressive forms in generative models, they all differ in their strength and are useful for different tasks. As generative models improve themselves with time it shows that they are likely to transform several industries including arts, healthcare, and data augmentation among others. Knowledge of the strengths and uses of every generative model type will help one to maximize the models' possibility in practice.

3.3 Applications of Generative AI

Generative AI is a relatively newly appeared and rather promising subbranch of AI that recently attracted much attention due to its ability to produce new content which is entirely indistinguishable from the data generated by an actual AI. The possibility and dexterity of generative AI is the flexibility and the ability of this AI in virtually any facet of our lives such as art, entertainment, health, and many others. All of these technologies are evolving year on year and utilizations are becoming more diverse by adjusting industries and revealing new avenues of development.

Generative AI has perhaps been most extensively brought to consumer's awareness most especially in the area of art. Here are some of the present and future applications of generative models: artists and designers employ generative models to discover new avenues for what can be created with art, music, and even writing. For instance, now one can speak about such technology as Generative Adversarial Networks (GANs) that can generate new types of painting; the model draws images as though they are a combination of several segments that an AI saw during the model's training. Similarly, in the growing world of music, compositions with the help of Artificial Intelligence, are also famous, and with the help of some specific formulas music of ages starting from classical to contemporary can be composed. These are not simply a new variety of inventions – these are new media of frontiers formed out of human creativity and code, intelligence as the artist's collaborator.

They affect people and their perception of media and entertainment in that people now receive media in a generative way from the generative AI. Nowadays, it is normal to see scriptwriters, story developers, as well as directors, employing AI models to compose scripts or even whole histories or whole scenes of movies and video games. To illustrate this, one can give some instance like in a video game, using artificial intelligence to develop images of environments and principal characters in the game would reduce the time and capital required to develop the game. Furthermore, such models are also able to generate several versions of a scene or dialogue so the best or the most appropriate one can then be chosen by the producers. In movie making, it has been used to erase aging from actors, produce realistic special effects, to give voice output from actors who died long ago meaning the prospects of freedom of creativity for moviemakers are vast. They not only contribute to enhancing the quality and the diversity of the offered material but also contribute to the studios making better material at a faster pace.

Nevertheless, the role of generative AI is also useful and great, especially in the field of healthcare whose utilization of generative AI seems to be revolutionary and extensive. One of them is the drug discovery industry – generative models are used to generate new molecules with certain properties and, maybe, new medicine. At the moment, AI means can, for example, propose through the analysis of wide chemistry files new molecules that can be used in the drug industry faster than the invention could take place if it were to be done manually. Indeed, generative AI is being employed to create realistic fake medical images for model training diagnostics. Such artificial images therefore eliminate the problem of lack of data, which is among the biggest challenges faced in medical research; it is also possible to feed a lot of diverse data into the AI-based diagnostic tools. This is particularly useful in such a field as radiology, where there is often a scarcity of big annotated images. Also, it becomes possible to use the AI-derived models to indicate, how the particular patient can respond to a certain therapy, which serves as the basis for the further evolution of the approach to corresponding patients in healthcare.

One rapidly growing area in the NLP is generative AI which already demonstrated significant progress with the use of such frameworks as GPT (Generative Pre-trained Transformer). With their help, it is possible to generate correct textual information that is meaningful and related to an ongoing conversation or a specific subject area, which distinguishes the manifestations of interfaces when using these models – starting from customer support services, and including creating texts for publications, and ending with interpreter services. For example, the generative AI in many applied platforms like bots develops intelligent interfaces capable of engaging in basic conversation, offering support in consumer relations, and answering questions or even providing suggestions. These conversational systems can also carry out multiple interactions simultaneously for further automation of several interfaces. In addition, generalization in chatbots can be achieved in content generation; it contributes to article writing, article summarizing, as well as writing of reports for journalism and business. Since A I can help with the creation of text-based content, organizations will be able to meet the expectation of delivering constant fresh information. Besides, generative AI models are being used for the creation of better and more efficient translation tools and ease the barrier of the language between people of different languages and different cultures. Another area or field in which generative AI is also emerging is the educational area, where it is being used to design personalized learning spaces. The generative models try to differentiate very important information on students that would assist in the formulation of lesson plans, exercises, as well as assessments to enhance learners' understanding. Education is thus individualized; there are noble gains that can emerge from such as each learner is supposed to be allowed to learn at his or her own pace to be well prepared to learn and probably master more. In addition, generative AI can produce new paradigms of education material in the form of virtual tutors and simulations that may improve the learning process of the students. These tools also can help teachers as the main part of administrative work will be done by AI, so teachers will be able to focus on the formation of efficient learning and student mentoring.

At the moment, generative AI is integrated into almost all the activities of a business such as content creation for marketing purposes, or improvement of supply chain logistics. For instance, they are now employed in the creation of digital marketing content for advertisement production; on-site and social media; as well as in email marketing. Given the fact that generative models consider the users' behavior, it can be possible to have content that is more relevant to the targeted buying behavior hence improving sales. Further, in the supply chain, that is generative AI is applied in demand prediction, stock management, and for portraying what-if segments and/or trends thus enabling companies to make improved decisions and to react to change.

AI also has apps in the financial industry, this has been applied in algorithm trading, credit risk assessment, credit risk management, and fraudulent practices. The algorithms applied in algorithmic trading are the capacity of the model to draw trading signals from data as well as other information obtainable from the past and the current market. All these strategies can be done unconsciously, thus making trading areas speedy, and effective, and bringing in profits, thus exploiting any opportunity within the market environment. In risk assessment, generative AI is used to generate several scenarios about the financial situation to identify potential risks and give recommendations to institutions on how they can efficiently handle their portfolio or finance. In addition, generative AI models are implemented to operate in fraud detection systems that discover certain patterns of behavior that depict fraud. As the data used can be updated daily these systems do not become obsolete through new threats and are capable of providing more accurate and timely alarms.

Nevertheless, it must be stated that generative AI and various solutions based on it also have disadvantages and questions of ethical profile which can be expected and should be considered thoroughly. The creation of these models to create authentic media content which in many cases are fake such as the deep fake models is a worrying factor to many people. As deepfakes can be utilized to provide the wrong information, identify people, and manipulate the crowd, deepfakes are hazardous to privacy security, and democracy. Moreover, we have still noticed some transitions in the copyright laws when it comes to AI writers, for there is often no evidence of who is or will be the author of the works produced by the AI. In addition, the widespread of generative AI also has certain implications that are averse to several industries and may cause numerous employees to become jobless such as industries of m&ent and customer relations. there is a great and broad scope of generative AI and requires new ideas in the various domains of implementation. From artistic and entertainment fields to health care, education, and business, generative AI is slowly but continuously transforming modes of work, people, and other entities – the 'products' in the so-called 'digital space'. Still therefore, however, as these technologies advance and develop, it is important to at least highlight the ethical and social implications of the subject matter and to capitalize on the opportunity of generative AI in the highest scope of societally beneficial. Generative artificial intelligence is going to be a great prospect but it should have all the safety measurements and legal consideration before it is going to be used for the welfare of the general public.

3.4 Evolution and Milestones in Generative AI

It is interesting to trace the development of generative AI as a result of the changes that have occurred in artificial intelligence and machine learning during the past decades. This field which has lately gained much attention can be traced to original concepts from mathematics, statistics, and computer sciences. Each generative AI progress is considered a technological innovation and a change in constructing, teaching, and employing AI systems. Probabilistic methods can be traced to the early development of generative AI, as well as the study of pattern recognition. Coming into the mid-twentieth century, several visions pointed to the future of the field that we now call AI. In AI's initial years the paradigm was more of symbolic or expert systems AI where information utilized rules and logical structures. However, when going through large volumes of unstructured data it was seen that these models were not very effective; which led to the use of probabilistic models and some of the earliest steps into machine learning.

The beginning of generative AI could be pointed to the creation of the Boltzmann Machine in the eighties by Geoffrey Hinton and Terry Sejnowski. The Boltzmann Machine is a kind of stochastic recurrent neural network and can learn and represent any kind of probability distribution. It was in this model that energy-based learning was first proposed where the system aims at minimizing the energy that corresponds to the probability of a given configuration of the inputs. While Boltzmann Machines were not very flexible and were difficult to train in practice due to computational restrictions, they serve as the basis of the next topics of development in generative models and provided some insight on how generative models could be created using neural networks with the integration of the statistical concept of data distribution.

The other complex architectures of the neural network appeared in the 1990s; at the same time, more computational power was available. It was during this time that the focus was shifting away from theoretical analysis of Machine Learning to primarily the application of the models themselves. The autoencoder was one of the important developments at this stage; it is a type of neural network that must learn a compact representation of data. Autoencoders contain an encoder that maps the input to a latent space of a lower dimensionality and a decoder that maps back to the original space. Autoencoder comprehensively was then used only for tasks like reduction of dimensionality and removal of noises in signal processing and so on, but later it transformed into more advanced forms like

Variational Autoencoders (VAEs) which are now at the heart of most modern generative AI.

The turning point that occurred in the development of generative AI took place in 2014 with the proposition of Generative Adversarial Networks (GANs) by Ian Goodfellow and his colleagues. In essence, GANs are a revolution in the capability of computers to synthesize new data. In the general architecture of GANs, there are two neural networks, one is called a generator, and the second one is a discriminator, both networks are trained simultaneously in a manner that could be compared with playing a specific game. The generator designs samples that are out of reality, and the discriminator, in contrast, assesses them versus genuine samples. The competition between these networks pushes the generator to generate realistic data samples, putting into evolution the technology of generative AI. They also provided a powerful instrument for generating high-quality images, music, and other types of data and stimulated a rapid increase in the amount of research and the scope of applications in creative and industrial fields.

As we have seen, GANs had a vast effect on the field and led to a sequence of technological developments in generative AI. Scientists extended the GANs' concept, using several types of GANs such as cGANs which generate data that depends on the input variables, and CycleGANs which translate one image to the other without having similar training examples. They brought a new scope for developing GANs from creative areas to applied utilities, such as in the medical field and data imitation.

Other major landmarks were reached with the advent of Transformer-based models, and more specifically the models designed for Natural Language Processing (NLP). The Transformer architecture was proposed by Vaswani et al. in 2017 and it was significantly different from most prevalent RNNs and CNNs. The former allows Transformers to model all the actions between all the tokens in the series at the same time which provides it a better capability to capture long-range connections. This innovation yielded models such as BERT namely Bidirectional Encoder Representations from Transformers and GPT which is short for Generative Pre-trained Transformer and performed better and made new records in several NLP tasks.

GPT is a language model by OpenAI that has revolutionized generative AI in the area of which is called natural language generation that aims at creating textual data that resembles that of human authors. GPT series including GPT-3, clearly showed it is possible to large pre-train models on large text corpus and then fine-tune them based on specific tasks. GPT-3 is a huge generative artificial model that under the scale of '175 billion parameters' can write sensible text on the context and uniface topicality and thus has excited and ignited interesting and timely debates on the applications and potential of

AI not just in generating text but in interactions and other fields as well. The use of Transformer models in NLP is also echoed by their application in other areas such as image and video generation even further widening the area of generative AI.

At the same time, other important steps were made, for example, in the development of a new type of generative model called Variational Autoencoders (VAEs). VAEs use elements of autoencoder, as well as probabilistic modeling, and tend to learn a factorial representation of the data so that the data can be generated from the output space. While GANs are concerned with generating output that is very 'realistic,' VAEs are intended to capture the distribution of the data, which makes them well-suited for problems that require output that is diversified and easy to explain. VAEs themselves and the work that has gone into integrating them with other generative models, for instance in the formation of hybrid architectures, have gone a long way toward increasing the 'general use' applicability of the generative AI field as a whole.

As generations evolve, there are always some issues that occur in generative AI. There are some problems associated with training such as instability in GANs training, Accidents in large models such as GPT-3, ethical concerns with AI-generated content, and so on. These difficulties, in turn, have incubated innovation, which resulted in the emergence of ways of stable training, effective architectures of models, and guidelines for the ethical application of AI.

It will also be seen that the evolution of generative AI is not just about achieving particular targets and goals; it is more than a technology; it defines a new era in artificial intelligence. The path of generative AI has also followed the general path of AI development, where each step forward unlocks new potential and new challenges at the same time. The future of generative AI looks way brighter and fresher with advanced research going toward the enhancement of the optimality, and effectiveness, along with the moral utilization of these potent generative models. Being already obvious in art, entertainment, and media, and being continuously developing in the healthcare field or in general, generative AI will only grow to become even more crucial to the contemporary digital environment.

3.5 Differences Between Discriminative and Generative Models

In the general field of machine learning two of the ideas that any learner should have an understanding of to understand how the discriminative and generative models read data are discriminative and generative models. As proposed, there are two kinds of models: data classification and learning from data Not surprisingly each imbues the task of learning from data with a highly distinct coloration, yet each has its advantages & liabilities. The discriminative and generative models' comparison can impact the effectiveness and the probability of the particular kind of machine learning solution that is to be applied based on the requirement of the relevant task.

Discriminative models are also often known as conditional models and the main goal of discriminative models is to give a probability of a label, conditional to some number of features. In other words, they begin learning at the frontier of the divide between one class of data and the other. This makes them especially useful in classification tasks where the main aim is to classify a given instance into a particular class of a given feature. In the classification problem, discriminative models that are most frequently implemented comprise logistic regression, support vector machine (SVM), and neural networks. Most of these models operate to estimate the decision surface and then use it to classify the data into different classes at the same time control the parameters in a bid to reduce the classification error in the training data set.

One of the main benefits of discriminative models for classification problems is the ability to resolve without complication. Discriminative models are often very accurate, particularly in areas where the largest concentration of the process is on the classification because that is the primary strength of discriminative models – to find the correct label for the data set in question. In comparison to generative models, such models are a bit more sparing in terms of computational complexity in the training phase as well as in their implementation. This is something they do not need, for only in that manner do they have to look at the boundary between classes in the space formed by the input features. Hence the discriminative models are used for activities like spam detection, image classification, speech recognition, and the like because here the endeavor is to classify the input data as accurately as possible.

As accurately as the channels, activities, and services have been classified and the boundaries of the classification defined, it has its disadvantages. In nearly all of the studied cases, discriminative models mark the fact that no assumptions have to be made regarding the distribution of the data. Originally introduced for classification purposes they are very accurate when defining classes but encompass do not encompass all structural characteristics of the given set. This can be somewhat restrictive if situations demand one to understand the generative model of the data. For example, discriminative models may fail in applications such as anomaly detection feature learning or learning about new features and generating new samples.

In contrast, the generative models' objective is to calculate the probability distribution of the features of the input and the label themselves. This means that they not only get the ability to segregate data into different classes but also receive an understanding of how data is produced. Generative models are therefore compound models that can be used in the performance of tasks such as classification, generation of new data, and outlier detection. A few of the most popular and basic generative models are; the Gaussian mixture models, the Hidden Markov models the modern advanced Variational autoencoder (VAE), and the generative Adversarial Network (GAN).

Like all the generative models, each of the models has this gotten ability to generate new vectors from the distribution of the primary data set. These make them very suitable for use such as image generation, text creation, or data expansion. For example, GAN used the creation of rather realistic pictures, which may be confused with the actual set of photographs, and VAE has made use of the generation of a great amount of data samples by sampling them from the learned latent space. They can also be used in any task that requires knowledge of the inherent distribution of data for instance in molecular design where new chemical molecules are developed based on the learned pattern of existing molecules.

This is why in the conditions when little or no labelled data is available at all, generative models are used instead. These models learn the joint distribution of the inputs and outputs so that they can take advantage of the structure of the data to perform well even where only a limited number of the labels are available making the models useful in semi-supervised learning paradigms. Also, viewing the structure of the data, the generative models can be used in cooperation with unsupervised tasks such as clustering or dimensionality reduction while they do not use annotations.

However, the capability of using the generative models brings additional costs that are associated with complexity and computation. It is very often that training generative model is more difficult than that of training discriminative models since it is estimating a joint probability distribution. This can be computationally highly intensive especially when dealing with high-dimensional data, this may need the use of advanced algorithms and high-end computational power. However, generative models can be problematic, for example by presenting a mode collapse problem, which means the model does not cover all the data diverse enough, or the problem of training VAEs because of the trade-off between the reconstruction error and the prior distribution in the latent variable space.

Moreover, deciding the interpretability of the generative models can be confusing compared to discriminative models as will be discussed below. Discriminative models give sharp decision boundaries that are straightforward to 'read', while generative models work by modeling the complete data distribution, thus are not as accessible. For instance, explaining the reason why a generative model has generated certain data could entail dissecting relations between the model parts, which is not easy.

It will be found that whether to use a discriminative model or a generative model completely depends on the task at hand. Discriminative models are therefore more suitable for tasks where the accuracy of classification is important and where the distribution of the data is of little consequence. Because they are efficient, easy to use, and designed to attain maximum prediction accuracy, they are also very useful in many real-life applications.

However, when the task is to identify the generative process of the data, generate new sample data, or work with situations where there is little labeled data available, then there are major benefits to using generative models. By putting it in position to model the joint distribution of inputs and outputs, generate realistic as well as using the structure of the data in semi-supervised, and unsupervised tasks can make them invaluable in more complex applications of machine learning.

Discriminative and generative models' comparison also draws attention to the current studies in machine learning that focus on merging the elements of both of these models. A special interest is being paid to the models that contain discriminative and generative components. Such models are created to retrieve the advantages of discriminative models such as efficiency and accuracy and, at the same time, include the usefulness and generative properties of generative models. For instance, semi-supervised GANs combine the generative ability of GANs with discriminative classifiers to enhance performance on tasks that have little labeled data.

Therefore, discriminative and generative models are two principles of learning from data that are distinctive but may be universal in certain aspects. Discriminative models perform well in those problems that involve the accurate categorization of items and are, as a rule, less complex in terms of training and understanding of the model's work. As generative models are more flexible, they are useful for data generation, understanding the data distribution, or when the labeled data is scarce. In the future, with the development of machine learning, there might be fewer qualitative differences between the mentioned models, while the subsequent development of new algorithms could inevitably lead to the best characteristics of both.

CHAPTER 4: HARDWARE FOR EMBEDDED DEEP LEARNING

4.1 Overview of Embedded Systems

An embedded system is a salaried systemization for computing that is used in particular mechanical or electrical operations. While PCs are multipurpose devices used for virtually any task and in almost any environment, embedded systems are used for only one or a few very special tasks and often have strict deadlines. They are used in nearly all the present-day gadgets right from home appliances to industrial machines where they offer essential services in a small, easy, and effective way.

So, in a way, an embedded system is a microcontroller or microprocessor, memory, and input-output interfaces. The microcontroller or microprocessor is the system CPU (Central Processing Unit), which runs the software that governs the system's operation. Data storage is a brief type of memory on the other hand comprised of both volatile memory like RAM and fixed/permanent storage like flash memory and holds program code alongside data expected during processing. I/O interfaces are used to interface the embedded system with other devices, sensors, or other related actors within an environment thus allowing it to take in inputs from the environment and also control the related functions in the environment.

 Most of the embedded systems are a combination of hardware and software, in their design and implementation. In addition, based on its application, hardware has to be developed for the specific tasks that the system has to accomplish, and more often than not, special circuits or other components may be needed to meet certain performance levels, power consumption, or physical size, among others. On the software side, the applications in embedded systems involve real-time operating systems (RTOS) or bare metal which implies that the application has to be responding to the tasks with relatively low delays and respond to timing constraints appropriately. The software has to be optimized because, being embedded systems, they are frequently characterized by several constraints and need to provide high reliability and non-error-prone operation.

Another general feature of embedded systems that applies to the majority of them can be mentioned as the integration of the system into a larger system. These are not on their device but rather they form part and parcel of a system in which they serve a particular purpose which is to aid the overall function of the device. For instance, in a current car model, some of the responsibilities of the embedded systems include engine control, braking system, as well as information entertainment. All of these systems are run separately but they all have to comply with others to provide the adequate work of the car or its safety.

As depicted in 5 above there is an array of uses and various industries use embedded systems. In consumer electronics, the application of the embedded system is seen in more extensive usage in devices ranging from smartphones, smart TVs, and home automation systems among others. These systems address every ranging from user interface to network connectivity as well as multimedia processing. In the field of medicine, they are applied in devices like pacemakers, insulin pumps, and diagnostic tools wherein a high level of precision and performance is vital for patient safety and care. Industrial automation also incorporates normally the use of embedded systems in robotics, process control, and monitoring systems that are used to increase the efficiency of processes in the manufacturing industry.

In telecommunication specifically, embedded systems are very vital to controlling the equipment in the networks as well as communications protocols. This common computing devices as routers, switches in addition to base stations are instances of devices that make use of embedded systems to sort the physical transfer of information alongside the arranging of signals. As with Aerospace and defense industries avionics, navigation systems, and unmanned vehicles where embedded systems perform high-end computation simultaneously to respond to the mission and safety concerns.

The change in embedded systems has been viewed in terms of microelectronics and system integration, software engineering, and integration systems. Over the years, development in technology has advanced the design of embedded systems with higher computation abilities, large memories, and better connectivity channels. The marked evolution of the SoCs is another testimony of this evolution since they are single chips with integrated Client/Server, including the CPUs, memory, and peripheral interfaces. More notably, SoCs foster enhanced simple and power solutions and hence meet the demand of the current embedded applications.

Wireless integration of embedded systems with the ability to interact with other applications in the internet space has also increased features and their functionalities. Networked IoT-enabled embedded systems are the modern reality given by the impact of the Internet of Things on the function of complex devices. With the help of IoT and embedded systems, data can be gathered and shared in real-time that results in possible advancements in smart home systems, industrial IoT, and connected healthcare systems. These systems involve intelligent and self-contained systems with sensors, communication interfaces, and algorithms for signal processing.

However, several challenges are associated with embedded systems which designers need to overcome. Thus, one of the major concerns is energy efficiency, especially taking into consideration that many embedded systems are used in cases where power supply is limited or is supplied through battery sources. The best practice is to report the current status of the batteries and the systems to optimize their power usage and have minimal need for maintenance and battery replacement. Furthermore, reliability and robustness are important too especially in areas where incorporated systems can lead to calamity. Due to the stringent requirements of the usage environment which include temperature fluctuations, mechanical stress, and electromagnetic interference, proper accommodations have to be made during the design of embedded systems.

Security is overall another major issue that affects embedded systems especially those that are interconnected and that connect to more extensive networks. Some of the risks associated with vulnerabilities in embedded systems are that they can jeopardize the whole system or network in which it is installed; thus, any protective mechanisms should be viable. This entails the use of in-house coding procedures employments of encryption features, and regular release of new software that may offer protection from existing and future vulnerabilities and hacks.

The subject of embedded systems is very complex and has an interdisciplinary approach to its development which consists of elements of hardware and software engineering and system integration. Regarding performance considerations, engineers and designers need to take into account the basic principles of operation, cost controllers, and environmental conditions to come up with the right embedded solutions. Simulation, prototyping, and repetitive or cyclical designing reduce the risk of having the embedded systems perform as required and in the ways for which they were designed.

Embedded systems are a crucial part of the present-day technologies that perform major operations in different applications. Due to their specificity, incorporation into more extensive systems, and capacity to perform under profound limitations they are invaluable in consumer electronics, medical technology, industrial applications, telecommunications, and numerous other domains. Due to the advancements in technology, embedded systems are bound to advance expanding their application domain and improving on the existing systems and equipment.

4.2 Processing Units: CPUs, GPUs, TPUs, and NPUs

Processing units are believed to be at the heart of the present day's computing systems due to their many calculations apart from other tasks. Different forms of processing units are available including

Central Processing Units, Graphics Processing Units, Tensor Processing Units, and Neural Processing Units, and the differences in their performance rely on the task that it is assigned to perform. It is therefore important to point out the features, strengths, and employability of those processing units regarding every computation type.

It is most often called the 'heart' of the computing system since it controls the entire computing system, this is where the Central Processing Unit is normally located. It has to carry out several tasks, which include, executing instructions that the system software has provided, manipulating and calculating data, and controlling the flow of data in the computer. As for the type of instruction, CPUs have flexibility and are of general use; they help handle a set of commands. They are usually comprised of several cores, which enable them to do different tasks at the same time. There are other functionalities like pipeline, out-of-order execution, and branch prediction amongst others that are incorporated in current CPU architectures.

Concerning me, it is imperative to point out that CPUs are presupposed for tasks, which require single-threaded sufficient performance and decision-making. These outshine in the execution of typical I/O operations and contain operating systems, productivity utilities, and Web browsers too. Besides, they are adaptable and their work may encompass a range of operations including databases, enterprise applications, and virtualization among others. Unlike vertical markets, they are irreplaceable for consumer and enterprise computing flexible and generally applicable solutions. Fig.

On the other hand, Graphics Processing Units or GPUs are processors that were developed to work in the graphical manufacturing industry and the management of graphical data information. GPUs were originally SIMD, which entails having a large number of less specialized cores that can do multiple operations at the same time. This parallel architecture or hierarchical matrix makes the GPUs more appropriate for handling large-scale data computations such as image and video processing, simulation, and machine learning among others.

Innovations including machine learning and artificial intelligence have unraveled the utility of GPUs in boosting operations that require extensive computational algorithms. For instance, training deep neural networks involves a lot of data processing, and this always requires computation of matrix operations, such tasks are always best handled by GPUs because of the aspect of parallelism. Thus, there is a great demand for GPUs among machine learning researchers and developers due to the enhancement in the training time and more number of models.

TPUs are an extension of processing units that are specific to Google's machine learning frameworks.

Before proceeding let me remind you that TPU is optimized for tensor computations which are essential in most of the neural network-based architectures. Unlike the usual microprocessors and graphics cards which are general-purpose auxiliary chips, the TPUs are specifically designed and implemented to execute/repeat the mathematical operations most commonly in the training of and in making use of neural networks and other architectures.

They are high-performance co-processors that interact closely with the host CPU to accomplish captures and matrix multiplications into tensors. They are used on a rather large scale by various Google services of the cloud machine learning kind such as the Google Cloud Machine Learning Engine as well as in the performance of many an AI model owned by the company. Designed for high utilization in the training phase as well as in the inference phase, our TPUs are built to accommodate large-scale usage. The variation is kept to a minimum and its architecture has many elements such as high-bandwidth memory and custom-built hardware acceleration which makes them high performers.

Neural Processing Units or NPUs are the other kind of specialized processors that are designed for improving artificial intelligence and machine learning operations. NPUs are directly opposite of TPUs as TPUs are meant for the calculations of neural networks while NPU architectures can be generalized and be used for any type of AI load. NPUs are used in various applications such as in mobile devices and edge computing systems, where efficient and high-performing executions of AI computations are characterized.

NPUs are presented as highly efficient devices with rather low latency in inference tasks. Some of them are built for low-power consumption devices such as smartphones, smart cameras, and other edge devices that employ real-time Artificial Intelligence such as image recognition, commanding voice, and natural language understanding. The NPUs include matrices of vectors for computation, activation functions, or other elements of the NN; for this reason, units tend to draw less power while running at high frequencies.

Besides, CPUs, GPUs, TPUs, and NPUs operate in different ways at the basic level, The following is that each processing unit is different from the other; These processors apply widely, and are unqualified – that is, they are suitable for most computation issues. GPUs are meant for parallel computing and are fast in tasks like graphics processing and artificial substantiation. These systems are these, TPUs work as tensor processors for large-scale machine learning tasks, and NPUs provide efficient AI inference at the edge.

This means that the processing unit to be used depends on the specific need of the application or workload in the case of the computer. In scientific computing as well as other tasks that require high levels of decision-making, CPUs are used instead of GPUs. In large-scale data processing i. e. big data processing as well as in parallel computing, the use of GPU results in enhanced performance. TPU is best suited for deep learning performance in the cloud network while NPU is fit for edge devices and mobile projects.

The major change in the processing units indicates that the market calls for diverse processors to cater to the ever-varying demands of computers today. The evolution of new material technologies, new architectural designs, and new integration approaches are quite effective giving improvements in performance, power usage, and versatility of all kinds of processing components. From experience, the processing unit has always been an important part of the development of new technologies, and with the change in computational needs and with the coming up of more uses for the technology, it can be seen that processing units will continue to have a big part to play in the future technologies and different areas.

Once again, we have understood the fact that there are several ways of performing a computation- using CPU, GPU, TPU, or NPU- each with its advantages and applicability. Whereas CPUs have a holistic and all-purpose computing processing capacity, GPUs have a specific focus on parallelism processing and machine learning boosting authority. TPUs are built for tensor operations for huge scale data of Artificial Intelligence whereas NPUs are built for AI computation in Edge and mobile devices. But the most important aspect of being aware of these units and their working is that it can aid selection of the right hardware as per some of these operations and further optimize the like operations in different types of systems.

In the domain of computing, Processing elements are general-purpose components that are used to do computing and computations. It should be mentioned that there are two basic types of these units, and there are more specialized versions that can be used at best in specific tasks. Some of them include; the Central Processing Unit (CPU), Graphics Processing Unit (GPU), Tensor Processing Unit (TPU), and Neural Processing Unit (NPU). All these processing units have different characteristics and ability to perform different tasks hence useful to do particular tasks.

They are commonly referred to as microprocessors which are derived from the term 'micro computer', Since its inception, the micro CPU has become the most versatile and the most regularly used computer chip in computer technology. They are supposed to perform different tasks which comprise running operating systems and applications, handling inputs/outputs operations, and computation tasks. CSPs are improved and optimized for single-thread procedures and they run well in sequences, decision-making movements, and dependable sequences. The existing generation microprocessors are equipped with more than one core, which means it has one or more processing units that can simultaneously execute several instructions and thus several operations at the same time to increase the level of performance. Among the components that are in the architecture of CPUs, there are high clocking rates, large cache as well as superior branch predictors among others.

Copus, on the other hand, are very easy to use but are not as elastic as the full-blown COPs and are not best fitted for parallel processing like major number crunching and graphical calculations. Well, we do not have to do that because here we have the Graphics Processing Units (GPUs). Originally designed for enhancing image depiction and video Control: Making HDR Gate Work on Various Screensos processing in graphic demanding functions, up-to-date GPUs have been evidenced to be efficient parallel processors that can compute several complicated operations. Unlike the current market CPU's which are optimized for single-thread performances, the GPU has thousands of uncomplicated cores for multiple threads. This architecture makes the GPUs especially optimized for applications where there is a degree of parallelism as in the following; scientific computations like simulations, artificial intelligence, and data processing.

It moves from GPU utilization only for image processing to general-purpose computing due to the ability of their capacity to accelerate operations that can be parallelized. For instance, in machine learning, GPUs are preferred for deep neural networks for the following reasons; Large datasets contain data in chunks that can be processed in parallel and this enhances the training of the networks. There are other frameworks for the execution of general-purpose applications which has been developed like CUDA (Compute Unified Device Architecture) to exploit the full capability of GPU for applications excluding graphics.

 Another type of Internet processing unit is called Processing Unit abbreviated as TPU which is specifically involved in improving machine learning operations. TPUs is the name that is short for Tensor Processing Units that are well suited for tensor calculations which are at the heart of deep learning algorithms; TPUs were created by Google. Another type of data structure that is more general than vectors and matrices are tensors and they represent the data and the parameters of the neural networks. The Palm calculations could also be conducted optimally as TPUs are characterized by high throughput of matrix computations and therefore may be beneficial, especially while training or even during the inference of deep models. Cu does this through hardware components e. g., matrix multiply engines that help in performing computations including the matrix multiplications that are inherent in neural network operation.

As it was stated in previous sections TPUs are intended to be used in machine learning and they offer some advantages in terms of performance and efficiency compared to other available accelerators. Therefore, by using customized hardware, TPUs can achieve a better throughput compared to GPUs and are almost near to it in terms of low latency. They also have such features as high bandwidth memory and interconnects which when incorporated, enhance the performance of these GPUs especially for large-scale machine learning tasks. TPUs are used massively in Google's cloud ML services with the chip made available through the Google Cloud Platform that has extended to various applications including natural language processing, image recognition, and recommendation systems.

Neural Processing Units (NPUs) are the other type of exclusive processing components meant to increase artificial intelligence (AI) potential and machine learning. NPUs are pre-programmed depending on the operations that are attributed to neural networks, and these include matrix operations and convolutions as well as activation functions. Email Tripathi and Rahul have compared NPUs to TPUs where TPUs are developed by Google while NPUs are manufactured by different companies and are part of smartphones and tablets, canted as embedded systems, and others. NPUs are designed for AI calculations, which bring high performance with efficiency making NPUs ideal for edge computing which is power-sensitive.

NPUs are also present in SoC designs which correspondingly means that they might cooperate with other processing units such as CPUs and GPUs in a single architecture usually present in the SoC architecture. It also enables one to optimize how AI operations are executed and at the same time take optimal advantage of the various processing units, in the handling of the various facets of an ML app. For instance, an integrated NPU smartphone means that permits all the functions including real-time image, voice recognition, and all other AI-related features with minimum power consumption rate and high performance.

In that case, again the choice remains with the user and/or the system designer whether to use the CPU, GPU, TPU, or the NPU based on the demand of the job and the conditions that surround the application. There are several applications where microprocessors are most suitable: low-level computing those that are conducted at the program level as well as those which consist of many decision-making operations that occur consecutively. GPUs are used for parallel computations which include graphical computations as well as handling large volumes of data which makes many threads beneficial to use. As much as TPUs are not one-click solutions they are designed for the machine learning workloads that provide high throughput especially required for deep learning. GPUs, on the other hand, will assist in enhancing the computation of AI in numerous existing applications that reach the mobile and embedded systems level and NPUs are designed to handle AI use cases in edge devices.

Each of these processing units is very important in developing the technology and extending the range of uses. The integration of processing units shows the ever-growing demand for unique processors that adapt to the ever-evolving stresses of traditionally multifaceted workloads. Prospects for the future are in anticipation of the emergence of new architectures and innovations that will advance the capabilities of the processing units and make a positive impact mainly in areas such as artificial intelligence, data science, and computational research.

Hence, we have CPUs, GPUs, TPUs, and NPUs into which the advanced systems can be classified; each with its efficiency, objectives, and utilization. While CPUs are general-purpose and give a high single-thread performance, GPUs are designed for high amounts of parallel computing, TPUs are built for high throughputs of machine learning, and NPUs are optimized for AI workloads at the edge. It is crucial to evaluate the potential of various types of processing units and extract their features for choosing suitable hardware for the selected application and for taking maximum benefit from the tailored elements of the up-to-date computing technologies.

4.3 Memory and Storage Considerations

Memory is an essential and functional aspect of computing systems, affecting the computing performance and its capabilities. Though all of these elements are related they each fulfill a specific role and have their specific matters to consider. It evaluates memory and storage requirements and their optimization critical to meet important application requirements and to protect data integrity.

Memory is also known as RAM (Random Access Machine); it is the space that a market uses to store data that is currently being processed or utilized. Every program is stored in storage media such as a disk which is later fetched into the memory during its execution so that the CPU can easily access it. This temporary storage is very important for the function of applications involved in programs and application execution since the read and write capabilities are fast and a core function in processes and tasks.

Organ memory has capacity and speed and directly affects the system speed of the devices. Additional RAM means more processes can be run at one time and means the computer can support more intensive software without lagging. This is particularly essential where there is massive data input, detailed modeling, or great workload demands. For example, in scientific computing or graphic designing, where large amounts of data are required to be processed there can be a marked improvement in the performance if adequate RAM is available and if we do not encounter a RAM bottleneck.

Furthermore, the intricacies of memory also incorporate its clock speed and bandwidth by which data can be accessed and manipulated. Quicker reading enables faster retrieval of data that make up the system and therefore enhances system performance. Other aspects of the architecture of memory also contribute to performance including, latency as well as type of memory for instance DDR4 and DDR5. In general use, high I/O boards as gaming PCs, servers, and others may incorporate superior memory to meet their performance demands.

Storage can also be defined as where data is stored for long-term use or is stored permanently. While memory tampers with and opens its content to the surrounding environment and loses this content each time that power is shut down, storage does not allow this content to be interfered with and makes it available as soon as is required. The two main categories of storage drives are hard disk drives popularly known as HDD and the other is solid-state drives commonly referred to as SSDs. HDDs employ spinning disks and read/write heads to store information whereas SSDs employ flash memory, which makes it easy to retrieve information much faster and with less chance of failure.

SSDs are growing popular day by day because of many advantages over conventional HDDs. It boots a computer faster, transfers files faster, and improves the overall performance of a computer which results in faster data access. As mentioned earlier, SSDs also do not include any rotating components; thus, they are less likely to feature mechanical failure than HDDs. This is particularly relevant in portable devices and any other working environment that requires the equipment to have some measure of shockproofing.

For selection between SSDs and HDDs, the following factors should be put into consideration; the kind of performance that is required in the gadget, the cost to be incurred, and the storage space needed. Cost-wise SSDs are slightly costlier per Gigabyte as compared to HDD but the performance and reliability are unimaginable for high I/O operations. Unlike the former, the latter has higher capacities at comparatively lower cost, which makes them useful in applications that involve mass storage, at low cost, for instance in archival systems or backup solutions.

Another aspect of storage is Hybrid Storage Solutions in which some of the advantages of both SSDs and HDDs are attained. Such configurations are usually composed of an SSD that serves as a cache or performs other intensive operations while the main storage on an HDD is provided. This approach can gain a balance of performance and cost, and many consumer and enterprise systems use this approach.

Memory and storage management is also important for sustaining the system's efficiency and the data they hold. Effective management entails making the best use of memories and especially storage to maximize them and utilize them effectively. To this end, memory paging and caching are some of the strategies that are used to optimize efficiency and obtain minimal response time. Memory management systems aim at the facilitation of the resources for active processes while at the same time minimizing the effects of the management to overbearing effects on the whole system.

In storage, there is a concern about data compilations and arrangements or means of alphabetizing the files. File systems like NTFS and ext4 or any other file systems for that matter offer the superior structure by which data storage devices are managed. Some of the basic care operations include defragmentation of hard disk drives and firmware updates of the solid-state ones. Further, the question of data backup, retention, and data protection from loss should also be cordoned off and effective solutions employed.

This has also changed how data is stored and shared, especially with the development of cloud storage and NAS solutions. Cloud storage is the utilization of outsourced large-scale storage services that are capable of being accessed through the web. This model has relative flexibility and convenience but brings certain issues into account including data security and privacy as well as network availability. NAS devices, on the other hand, are networked storage where multiple users or devices within a network can have access to the data stored in the NAS devices making them ideal for shared workspaces or when multiple users and or devices are going to require access to the same data.

New storage technologies that are in the market include the NVMe storage and 3D NAND flash that are pulling the performance and storage capacities of devices to the next level. NVMe for instance, is a data transfer interface for storage devices that provides even higher data transfer rates than traditional interface methods and has lower latency than NVML, which in turn boosts the SSD performance. 3D NAND is a form of enhancing storage density where the cells are stacked vertically and this has the role of increasing the amount of storage capacity as well as the reliability of the flash technology used.

Memory and storage are basic modules in computer systems with each having a unique function in computation and should be handled with much attention when it comes to computing system design and space allocation. Memory is a system that offers fast access to data that is necessary for a short time and Storage as a system that offers permanent data storage also contribute to the system's performance and functionality. New developments have remained to enhance both fields providing chances of making greater enhancements aimed at meeting the modern age demands of applications. Memory and storage, as separate resources need to be well-managed to design effective, reliable, and high-performance computers.

Memory and storage are among the most vital sub-systems of computing systems and have a close relation to the computing and efficiency of the devices. The distinction as well as factors for selecting and optimizing both memory and storage are important in designing optimal computing systems. Memory and storage, as we know, share the same name when referred to in everyday language, but they are completely different from each other and have different features such as speed, capacity, and volatility.

Memory or as commonly known as Random Access Memory (RAM) is another important component of computing systems that work alongside the processor to store data and instructions required by the processor at any one time. RAM is optimized for rate; it makes the data easily available to the CPU needed in executing tasks. This speed is crucial for processing and performing tasks within a limited period so that it can have access to data that can further be manipulated. RAM is volatile which implies that, when power is switched off, then it will lose all the information stored in it. Due to this volatility, RAM is not useful for data storage in a long-term manner but it is very suitable for short-term data storage when data is very active in computation.

The units of RAM in a system greatly determine the rate at which the system will perform its operations. A lack of RAM can cause the computer to run comparatively slower and more often than not, the system begins to use the hard drives or SSDs as virtual RAMs when the actual RAMs are full. This is why a user needs to have a sufficient amount of RAM to avoid stutters and especially for applications that require a lot of RAM such as video editing, gaming, virtual machines among others. Current PCs are fitted with several gigabytes (GB) of RAM, with performance-optimized computers having even the capacity for extensive RAM.

On the other hand, Storage is defined as the creation of the records especially to archive or long-term data storage. On the other hand, storage can be defined as a medium in a system that holds data in a non-volatile nature, in other words, data stored in storage cannot be lost if the power is removed from a computer system. There are quite several storage types, and this will be discussed with their differences as well as their applications. HDDs and SSDs are the two primary storage forms used in modern systems in this paper, The differences between HDDs and SSDs will be analyzed.

 HDDs are the conventional storage devices in which, data retrieval and writing are done on spinning magnetic disks. It's because of their capability to store big volumes of data and their relatively cheap cost per gigabyte. There is the fact, that HDDs are usually slower than SSDs because of the physical process that is happening inside an HDD. The read/write speeds of the current HDDs are fixed by the capacity and speed of the disks spin and the read/write electromotor heads. This makes HDDs less preferable for such use because access to data in HDD takes a relatively longer time compared to SSDs thus making it harder to boot an operating system or to load large files as quickly as it would take with an SSD.

 Unlike, hard disk drives, SSDs make use of flash memory for storing data as they have faster access times and data transfer rates. To refresh, HDDs have a mechanical structure that includes the spinning platters and the actuator arm while in SSDs case, there are no such components since they rely on semiconductor technology to store data. The advancement in the SSDs means the system will boot faster, the file transfer rate will be faster and the overall responsiveness of the whole system will be enhanced. The application of SSDs is dominant and constantly growing in consumer devices like laptops, PCs, and other devices because their performance is incomparable and more reliable than HDDs.

When it comes to choosing the right kind of storage, one has to consider capacity and performance as important factors to base one's judgment on. The given storage capacity of a device defines the amount of data that it is capable of storing, the larger the storage capacity the number of files, applications, and media that can be stored is large. Most users balance between SSDs and HDDs in which the SSD is used as the primary drive for the

Operating System and the most used applications while the large capacity HDD is used for storage of other data that may not be frequently used or backed up.

In addition to the conventional HDDs and SSDs, there are other innovative technologies including NVMe and U. 2 interfaces. NVMe is an interface that aims to make use of the high-performance features of today's SSDs by directly accessing the PCIe bus. This leads to an even higher rate of data transfer than the SATA (Serial ATA) SSDs that were hobbled by the older SATA interface. Indeed, the NVMe SSDs are quite advantageous, especially for those that involve heavy workloads and environments that need frequent access to data like gaming and professional use.

Another factor is "storage capacity" for which cloud storage solutions provide solutions that are scalable and remotely accessible. Cloud storage solutions give the user the capability to store data on online servers with options to access such information on any other device connected to the internet. Cloud storage may be cheaper than other ways of data management as the providers offer different levels of storage space depending on the client's requirements. However, the use of cloud storage has had some pros but it comes with cons such as security privacy, and internet bandwidth.

Other parameters besides capacity and performance are the integrity of the data and their redundancy levels. Data integrity makes certain that the stored data do not get corrupted with time as they are retrieved and used for other activities such as calculations. Applying measures that make several duplicates like RAID (Redundant Array of Independent Disks) will increase data protection since data will be stored on different disks and in case of disk failure, data will be recoverable. Some of the preferred configurations include RAID 1 where data is copied to two different disks for purposes of mirroring as well as RAID 5 which provides both disk striping and disk parity.

Memory and storage management are all about the trade-off between speed, storage capability, and expense. For instance, in a server environment the memory and storage can hence be optimized to enhance the processing power and the manner information is dealt with. Other optimization methods that may help to increase throughput and keep costs under control include memory caching, data compression, and storage tiering. Caching on the other hand is the ability to keep much-used data in higher-speed memories to lower the access time, whereas data compression is the act of lowering the amount of storage required by files and storage tiering is the utilization of different types of storage hardware depending of the access rate and performance requirement.

All in all, memory and storage are two fundamental elements in computing systems where each plays a different role and has different features. RAM is another important form of memory, which is comparatively faster and used to store data temporarily, which is actively in use at any given time, while storage devices like the Hard disk drive (HDD) and solid-state drives (SSD) are used for the permanent storage of data with differing storage space capabilities and speeds. It is crucial to learn the features that distinguish these constituents and be able to make correct decisions when defining their deployment and usage to achieve the most effective consequence in system performance and data management. Continually, new advancements in memory and storage technologies will progress the computing systems, and subsequently, advance other applications and industries.

4.4 Power Efficiency and Thermal Management

Some of the problems associated with modern computing frameworks are energy intake and dissipation, heat dissipation along with its impact on performance, reliability, and power consumption. As the improvement in the technologies goes on such devices are used more often as they offer great output, power utilization, and cooling systems. Appreciation knowledge of the specific challenges of power efficiency and thermal management and the strategies and Technologies EMPLOYED to enhance these two areas of conductor knowledge.

Computational efficiency on the other hand is a measure of the ability of the computing system to render its computational services with the least electrical power. Battery life control is not only relevant to the battery life of mobile phones and laptops but also to cost and energy efficiency as well as computer recycling in large-scale data centers and other similar applications. Low power consumption makes it possible to save energy hence being friendly to the natural environment other than cutting costs of operating a business.

As has been indicated power optimization is one of the key approaches and one of the key things in this area is to optimize the hardware. As for power management, they are both designed for that or have properties for altering the performance according to the power usage of the CPU or GPU. Other techniques like Static and Dynamic voltage and frequency scaling (DVFS) enable such processors to adjust the voltage as well as the frequency of their operations depending on the task at hand implying that they consume less power during the idle time. Power gating is another which is seen where an entire slice of a processor is put off when idle, which helps in saving power. These adaptive mechanisms help in controlling the performance with power consumption and therefore, the time of operation of the system.

Another equally important factor that supports power management is software optimization. Some of the methods, which may be implemented in an attempt to reduce power consumption may be coupled with proper coding styles and methods, compactness of algorithms, and compactness of the schedule of the events. For instance, low-step algorithms which discard computations that add no value hence saving on energy. The operating systems and applications with sophistications, which allow the control of power such as disabling the inactive portions and putting them to sleep, or executing a program at a time of minimal use of computer resources, boost system power. These presented soft computing techniques allow the developers and the system administrators to gain significant power savings.

 Thermal control is also the process of governing the heat generated by computing elements to prevent overheating and a consequent deterioration of the same. Here, thermal management is of utmost importance to make the hardware more robust and long-lasting since heat is lethal to the systems. Every time the technology in these computing devices is advancing with the devices being more powerful and even compact, it becomes a challenge to deal with heat.

Heat is mainly generated in processors, memory, and the other parts of the computer that require a relatively high-power consumption during computation. To cope with this heat, several cooling methods are employed and among them are as follows; The most popular methods used by people include heat sinks and fans and among the most common ones. An example of a heat sink is defined as a cooler device, which is utilized to determine the heat losses of the critical parts. They are mostly made up of substances with higher thermal conductivities than that of heat; the metals used include aluminum or Copper; the other part is quite large so that it can expel the heat. Often, blowing or fan units can be incorporated with heat sinks, and the fans are used to circulate the air surrounding the heat sink to enhance the rate of cooling.

Consequently, various cooling methods are used in high-performance computing systems. Impaired heat dissipation is experienced in the following components: A liquid cooling system is a method of using a liquid coolant that acts as a medium of absorbing heat from the components and then expelled to a radiator where it is converted to vapor and dispensed into the environment. Appropriate for increasing power density or for boosting such systems to such a density liquid cooling is better suited to air cooling. This technique is widely adopted in gaming PCs, servers, and workstations whereby better heat dissipation is mandatory.

Another measure known as the advanced technology of thermal management is the incorporation of Phase Change Materials (PCMs). They use the concept of phase change because they are capable of trapping and emitting heat. Thus, it can be concluded that with such materials, additional heat-insulating properties are implemented, and it will be possible to maintain suitable temperatures in the equipment when it is actively used for processing. PCMs are typically used as an addition to conventional cooling systems to enhance the heat dissipation performance of the system.

Another part of thermal management is controlling flows through the device during the work of the device. The constant complicated interrelationship of case design, operating space, and airflow characteristics dictates that hot air is expelled in the right manner and cold air is drawn into the case in the right manner. Hence when the engineer schedules the system to prevent putting essential devices in the regions of high temperatures, while? Conducting airflow in such a system one can prevent striking temperatures and as a result, manage to control the system from overheating.

Power efficiency and thermal management go hand in hand in a way that improving power efficiency also adds to the thermal aspect. Since power usage is low then so does the heat; cooling devices are also not under pressure and strain. On the other hand, efficient thermal control results in power retention and not compromised performance that has seen the clients set standards to reach the right temperatures.

Nevertheless, concerns about system power consumption and thermal control responsible for it are especially critical in mass data centers because of the large number of pieces of equipment and high energy costs. This is usually done by complex cooling like the hot/cold aisle containment where the equipment is placed and aligned in a manner that there is a hot aisle and a cold one. This also improves the cooling methods efficiencies and reduces energy use. Additionally, the components within the data centers that can vary may include energy-efficient parts, the power supply section, and the cooling systems which in turn raises the total facility power usage efficiency or the total facility energy use per energy used by IT equipment only.

An important factor for power usage and thermal management has been realized and pushed on further for more development of newer technologies and materials. However, with better Thermal Interface Materials, better cooling solutions, and in general better Semiconductor processes the latter problem has been researched to find a solution for the new advancement in computing. Such development will remain paramount to achieving the required performance as the device capability increases and the power consumption and heat generation increase.

Energy consumption rate and heat dissipation are crucial goals of today's processors in systems' architectures that define performance, durability, and energy efficiency factors. Optimizing power usage and controlling or minimizing heat results in better performance and longer life span of the hardware as well as reduced operating expenses. The effectiveness of the power consumption and thermal considerations underlines the necessity of design solutions integration and continuous advances in response to present and future computing requirements. It will be seen that in the development of the future of computing new developments in these areas will continue to be made as technology progresses.

Energy consumption in powerful computing systems including the data processing component is another important aspect of design and functioning as well as heat generated. They are indispensable in achieving optimal performance and in extending the life of a system as well as in considering the environmental aspect. With the evolution of technology in the field of computing, the problem of power and thermal management is even more crucial due to the present day's sophistication and high-power consumption of devices.

Power efficiency is defined as the capability of a computing system to work and solve needed tasks with minimal electrical power. Effective power management goes further in controlling electricity expenses that are incurred in operations while at the same time lowering the impact that technology has on the environment. Energy consumption is especially important in mobile solutions such as smartphones and laptops since battery longevity directly affects the customers' satisfaction. Through the efficiency of electricity utilization, these gadgets can work for long hours before they are recharged, thus making them more useful and portable.

The major sub-systems that influence power consumption include the processing unit, memory, and storage unit. Today's CPUs and GPUs come equipped with numerous power management mechanisms to ensure power control. For instance, the processors of these computers incorporate schemes such as dynamic voltage and frequency scaling (DVFS) to avoid applying constant power, voltage, and clock rates as may be necessitated by the demands of various tasks and applications. In a situation where the workload within a system is low and this is true for a long time, DVFS will reduce power consumption by decreasing the frequency and voltage of operation. On the other hand, if more performance is desired, then the system can increase the frequency and the voltage accordingly hence managing the power consumed according to the performance required.

Apart from DVFS, modern processors also use power gating as another technique of handling power. Power gating can be considered as another technique that refers to the switching off of power to the unused components or cores in the processor that contributes to leakage power and the total power of the processor. This technique is especially useful in multi-core processors where not all the cores available are needed at a certain time. The power and efficient utilization of the fabrication is optimized by turning off unrequired cores thus getting the best of it all without compromising on the performance of the system.

There are few areas where software has such a profound impact in terms of improvement in power efficiency. Work that is done involves reducing the number of calculations that need to be performed by the processor so that power consumption is minimized. Energy-wise systems and applications are those that display a high level of intelligence when it comes to power consumption. For example, power features in operating systems setups can 'park' non-active hardware structures and components or active system resources based on patterns of use. These techniques are software-based and additional to hardware power-saving features to obtain higher energy savings.

Whereas thermal management is more about the control and removal of the heat produced by the computing components. Thermal control is critical to system integrity and stability, and would significantly reduce the risks of thermal problems by preventing overheating. Heating is a natural process that occurs in any computer because various elements such as the processors, memory, and others consume electrical power and emit heat as a result. In case the laptop is not designed to dissipate heat adequately, heat can result in the throttling of the laptop's performance, system freezes as well as the reduction of the useful life of the various hardware components.

The most effective technique used in the management of heat in computing systems is through the use of heat sinks and fans. Heat sinks can also be described as passive cooling elements which have the capability of collecting and expelling heat from essential components. Heat sinks are constructed from metals that have a high thermal coefficient of expansion, and are available in a range of shapes, typically aluminum or copper, to increase the exposed surface area for heat loss. Heatsinks, when employed in combination with fans force air across hot components and in the process expel heat better. This maintains good operating temperatures and wards off, the effects of overheating through the help of heat sinks and fans.

For other types of high-performance computing systems such as gaming PCs and server PCs, enhanced cooling forms are used. Liquid cooling implies a process wherein a liquid coolant is used to take heat away from the components and transfer it to a cooler principally via a radiator. Liquid cooling provides a better way of cooling a system than air cooling since it addresses high power density or overclocked setups. This method is applied particularly in circumstances where optimum functionality and thermal dissipation are needed.

Another new concept in thermal management is phase-change materials or PCM for short. PCMs change their phases from solid to liquid and vice versa while storing and releasing heat in the process. These materials offer extra layering for thermal insulation to avoid overheating, especially after a period of high d activity. In situations where there are frequent changes in temperature and the need to manage temperature changes effectively then, PCM is particularly useful in managing such changes.

Air management is another thing associated closely with thermal management because it Also focuses on the convective cooling. Proper design of the case, proper location of vents, and airflow directionality are of uttermost importance to make sure the hot air leaves the system and cooler air is pulled in. Proper airflow distribution allows the avoidance of concentrated areas of heat and achieves a general and balanced temperature of components. This consideration is important in ensuring that the performance and reliability of the device is achieved especially when the form factor is a critical consideration that leads to the incorporation of miniaturized systems that make cooling a constraint. It is important to point out that the use of power-efficient components is strongly tied to thermal considerations. Observing this, power efficiency is also good for the management of heat dissipation so that it does not affect thermal management systems. On the other hand, poor thermal management detracts the power efficiency since the components are throttled back, and others are exposed to temperatures that are suboptimal for their function. Therefore, the interlink between power and thermal management techniques is critical in ensuring that high levels of performance and dependability of current computing systems are attained.

In data centers and large-scale computing power and heat management is even more important since there are many computing units fitted within a limited space. Hot and cold aisles are common in data centers where the cooling mechanism is conditioned to optimize the airflow through the aisles. This approach entails organizing the server racks in a way that hot and cold air streams are segregated in an attempt to cool the servers and minimize energy use. Data centers also use efficient code for every component, power supply units, and cooling systems that prevent excessive power consumption required for cooling the IT equipment; total building energy usage is the dependency on power using effectiveness (PUE), which is the overall ratio of the energy used by IT equipment alone.

The approach of energy conservation and minimizing heat production is also applied to current research activities related to the further development of technology. A diverse advancement in power and thermal management is observed in various material science technologies, semiconductor solutions, and cooling. These efforts are aimed at creating better and more efficient computing systems as well as providing necessary power consumption for the constantly developing and requiring more power applications.

Energy consumption and heat generation are other important features of current computer platforms that concern throughput, dependability, and ecological issues. Both power consumption and thermal management are efficient ways to make the systems perform better and make the lifespan of the hardware longer while minimizing the costs of carrying out operations. Thus, ordinary power savings, cooling systems, and other measures should be complemented with efficient practices in designs and development to meet these demands and further develop computer systems.

4.5 Popular Embedded Platforms: Raspberry Pi, NVIDIA Jetson, Google Coral

For flexible integration and cost-effective solutions with a high ability to solve specific problems, embedded systems have featured market flexibility. Now let's consider some productive working environments some of which are popularly known as embedded working environments such as Raspberry Pi, NVIDIA Jetson, Google Coral, and more. All these platforms have certain peculiarities in terms of the provided features and benefits and are usable in various capacities and fields such as in education, robotics, AI, or IoT.

At present, the most popular and well-known platform is Raspberry Pi which is rather cheap and has many fans. The Raspberry Pi was developed by a British organization known as Raspberry Pi Foundation and refers to a credit card-sized computer that can run various operating systems among which are Linux-based operating systems the most widely used operating system on this computer is the Raspbian OS commonly referred to as the Raspberry Pi OS. The greatest strength of the device is one which is readily apparent, its cost – which stands at $35 for the basic model aimed at hobbyists and engineers alike.

For the hardware, the circuit includes a Broadcom ARM-based processor, several Universal Serial Bus interfaces, a High-Definition Multimedia Interface, and the General-Purpose Input/Output pins. The GPIO pins make it possible for individuals to be able to use Raspberry Pi to interface with different sensors, actuators, and other accessories and therefore the Raspberry Pi is suitable for different sorts of home-based projects as well as learning purposes. It also comes with several related accessories and extensions such as cameras and a touch display making it even more flexible.

Of course, other than the use in the educational, and hobbyist, those projects have been implemented in many areas such as home automation, media centers, and even small-scale server systems. First, it is a low-power consumption device and small in size, so it can be easily used in projects that occupy small space and power. This is due to the vast number of audiences using this platform in the Internet arena and the availability of numerous tutorials and projects.

There is also another type of embedded board known as NVIDIA Jetson which is well-known for its focus on performability and AI. The Jetson family of AI is by NVIDIA with variations that consist of Jetson Nano, Jetson Xavier NX, and Jetson AGX Xavier among others. These platforms are for AI computing and machine learning, which makes them suitable for Robotics, Autonomous cars, and Smart cities.

The Jetson platforms are designed with NVIDIA-compatible GPUs; Cuda has the massive computational parallelism necessary for AI and deep learning. For instance, an entry-level Jetson Nano comes with a 128-core Maxwell GPU while Jetson Xavier NX and Jetson AGX Xavier come with Volta and Turing GPUs. These GPUs are capable of processing large and complex shallow and deep neural network models and real-time data processing which is of great importance for the target applications in image processing, natural language processing, and sensor fusion applications.

Another key aspect of the Jetson platform is that it comes with NVIDIA's Tensor RT as well as Deep Stream SDKs. Tensor RT differs from the other deep learning frameworks because it takes the trained neural networks and optimizes them to be faster in Jetson devices. Deep Stream is a platform to develop and run video analytics applications based on artificial intelligence and therefore aids in implementation creations such as smart video monitoring or self-driving.

One of the development tools and accessories in the development of the Jetson ecosystem is Jetpack SDK which has libraries, APIs, and sample code for software development. It also has a constantly evolving pool of developers and partners to work with AI applications and backing this up with forums, tutorials, and cooperation projects.

Coral from Google is a low-computing environment utilized by Google for building and running AI & ML models at endpoints. There are Coral products in the market, these include the Corona Dev Board, Coral USB Accelerator, and Coral Mini PCIe Accelerator. These are devices designed to be all about executing Machine Learning models at the operational level while not necessarily having to go to the cloud. This capability is really valuable in scenarios that require instant decision-making and where there is no breathing space as it were.

The Coral Dev Board is a computer-on-module developed from a single CPU ARM soc and also provided with Google's edge TPU for TensorFlow lite models. Edge TPU is an ideal solution for efficient inference with low power consumption, so the corresponding idea will work best in IoT smart cameras and other applications of edge computing. The Coral USB Accelerator is intended to make objects and devices AI-capable and the Mini PCIe Accelerator is prepared with the same function.

One of the unique features of Coral is that some of the used frameworks such as TensorFlow Lite, a Google proprietary framework for mobile and embedded devices which is incompatible with the Coral platform integration. Using TensorFlow Lite models, it is possible to create the models from the standard TensorFlow models, and also the models can be enhanced for execution on the Google Edge TPU. This makes it easy for developers to incorporate artificial intelligence for functions such as image processing, locating an object in the image as well as voice recognition.

Coral also has some of the Development Tools & Resources that include Coral API which can be useful in the integration of Artificial Intelligence aspects to the applications. From a user point of view, the amount of information and support that Google provides to the development community is an added advantage.

Summing up the Raspberry Pi, NVIDIA Jetson, and Google Coral are three mainstream embedded platforms with certain characteristics and advantages. Low cost and low power usage are the aspects of Raspberry Pi that make it fit for use in learning institutions and by enthusiasts. The NVIDIA Jetson platforms are specifically tailored for compute and interface AI applications and are characterized by a high degree of parallelism and abilities for complex ML tasks. Google Coral is an edge computing platform derived from Machine

Learning and Artificial Intelligence inference. Together, these sites are an extensive continuous range of the presence of embedded computing options regardless of whether it is an introduction lesson for microcontroller systems building and coding, Avnet advanced AI solutions set.

These embedded platforms become foundational to the construction of all kinds of applications in the Lego platform, from attempts taken on marginal projects to solid applications of the most complex. Among the most used ones are Raspberry, NVIDIA Jetson, and Google Coral. All these three platforms are meaningful and packed with features and capabilities that differ in the field concerning embedded computing and artificial intelligence.

Without a doubt, Raspberry Pi is probably one of the most recognized specific embedded platforms hitherto evident and feasible. Raspberry Pi is a credit card size low-cost computer initiated by the Raspberry Foundation and it is highly cherished by those people who find interest in electronics technology and many engineering students. It has been widely used due to its low cost, and versatility in its employment and it has greatly benefited from the support of a very informed community. Hence, the Raspberry Pi series incorporates models such as the Raspberry Pi 4, and Raspberry Pi Zero and all of them comprise specific performance and communications options.

An operating system for the device it produced known as Raspberry Pi OS earlier referred to as Raspbian, could also work on other versions of Linux and Windows 10 IoT core. It supports USB, HDMI, Hardware interface connection ports, and other connection types such as Ethernet and WiFi among others. This makes for very unlimited uses for several uses for instance in learning projects, home automation, and in the creation of prototypes.

A final and good advantage that is related to the Raspberry Pi is that the product has a good and large support base. This community hosts a variety of tutorials, projects, and software libraries that assist users to begin and also to solve any difficulty they come across. Cost and versatility are other uses of Raspberry Pi boards that are mainly used in Internet of Things projects, robotics, and media centers. GPIO pins available on the platform enable the platform to interface with several sensors and peripherals and this makes it very useful in embedded systems.

Another widely known embedded board is the NVIDIA Jetson which targets specifically the edge AI and High compute. High GPU-accelerated computing capability exists in the NVIDIA's Jetson series which includes Jetson Nano, Jetson Xavier NX, and Jetson AGX Xavier. These platforms are linked to the cores; for instance, NVIDIA's CUDA cores and Tensor cores provide high levels of artificial intelligence and machine learning algorithms.

The Jetson platforms are suitable for applications that require fast computational frequencies and processing them and these include; self-driving cars, robotics, and image and video recognition. It is important to understand that all the models in the Jetson series offer different performance and memory competencies making it ideal for use in simple projects, mid-raged projects as well as top-end industrial projects. For instance, the Jetson Nano is suitable for beginners in the AI domain but, the Jetson AGX Xavier is the flagship of NVIDIA's developer boards for AI targeted towards professional researchers and developers.

The last feature of the Jetson platform that should be mentioned is the integration into the rest of the software coming from NVIDIA. Some of them are as follows: JetPack which has developed the full tool suite for the software stack of AI diagrams and libraries of deep computers, visions, and multimedia processing. In addition, the easy availability of porting of serious frameworks including TensorFlow, PyTorch as well as OpenCV facilitates the developers to port also optimize the AI models on the Jetson platform.

Another noteworthy embedded platform is Google Coral which is intended to accelerate the assessment of the ML models at the edge. From Coral of Google, it was informed that the devices are built-in Edge TPU which is designed specifically for the execution of the model of TensorFlow Lite. The product segments already existing out there that have been developed by Coral include the development boards, USB accelerators, and the system on-modules and these will be very useful in the deployment of edge AI across the various fields.

The main selling point of Coral is that it seeks to accelerate all forms of ML on the device, and in its vicinity, thereby reducing dependence on cloud resources, and latency. This capability may be important especially for real-time image and speech recognition because the speed of the response may be valuable in such cases. This endows Coral devices with the capacity to make fast inferences and take low power, hence being appropriate for embedded systems.

Coral platforms are friendly with TensorFlow Lite, Google's tuning of the well-known TensorFlow structure that is intended for the running of ML models on edge devices. The above integration also assists in the simple deployment of the trained model to the Coral devices and further optimizing for the Edge TPU. Also, Coral offers different optical software aids and application programming interfaces such as Edge TPU Compiler and Model Maker for operating and implementation of machine learning solutions.

Thus, Raspberry Pi, NVIDIA Jetson, and Google Coral are three different but great computers for embedding and artificial intelligence. Raspberry Pi is much cheaper compared to PC, suitable in almost every aspect, and has a big society where people demonstrate their experience and projects, which is why; Raspberry is used in schools, people, and pilot designs. NVIDIA Jetson offers high computation and edge AI systems, featuring the industry's leading GPU-enabled boards for robotics, self-driving cars, and superior image recognition. The Google Coral is designed to work on the ML inferencing on the edge where it offers its Edge TPU for real-time AI solutions that consume little power.

These platforms demonstrate the further evolution of the range and potential of embedded systems, provide an appropriate solution for each of the tasks in a wide range of possibilities, and work on the advancement of the technologies. To learn or to prototype high-powered or deep learning platforms Raspberry Pi, NVIDIA Jetson, and Google Coral are handy devices for developers and engineers enabling the domain of embedded computing to evolve continually.

CHAPTER 5: SOFTWARE FRAMEWORKS AND TOOLS

5.1 Popular Deep Learning Frameworks: TensorFlow, PyTorch, MXNet

Deep learning has transformed several domains like computer vision, natural language processing, and robotics to bring changes across industries including, but not limited to, healthcare to self-driving vehicles. At the core of the continuous advancements in deep learning are these frameworks that allow people in the fields – researchers, developers, and practitioners – to build, train, and deploy their neural networks. TensorFlow, PyTorch, and MXNet are some of the most powerful deep learning frameworks that are practiced today. These frameworks have then entrenched themselves in the deep learning architecture each with different attributes and tools formulated to address various concerns.

TensorFlow is a deep learning framework and it has been developed by the Google Brain team. After its open-source release in 2015, TensorFlow has received appreciation and adoption due to its features like; scalability, and durability, coupled with a rich community. It offers an extensive environment for creating as well as implementing machine learning models for research, prototyping purposes, and highly scaled industrial purposes.

As for the advantages of TensorFlow, flexibility, and scalability can be regarded as primary. TensorFlow is suitable for a broad variety of machine learning applications; starting from basic feed-forward architectures and going up to more advanced models such as GANs and transformers. In this sense, its architecture is quite flexible and takes the opportunity to define models at several levels of abstraction. For instance, TensorFlow comes with Keras, a high-level API designed to ease the construction of neural networks through an interface that conceals most of the tensor operations. For the detailed work, TensorFlow enables the performing of low-level tasks that enable the fine-tuning of the models.

TensorFlow is quite powerful in its hardware compatibility, whether with CPU, GPU, or even the TensorFlow Processing unit. This makes it ideal for training models on large datasets on powerful hardware or applying models on mobile systems and other edge conditions where resources are limited. Google's integration of TPU has turned TensorFlow into the best choice for production systems where performance is critical.

Another factor attributable to TensorFlow's popularity is the community that has developed around it. Google and the TensorFlow community have made available comprehensive documentation and resources engaging tutorials and a diverse range of examples for using the TensorFlow framework for both novices and more experienced professionals.

Another important aspect of TensorFlow is that it also has a rich number of tools: TensorBoard, used for visualization of models, and TensorFlow Lite proposed for use on mobile and embedded platforms. These tools enable the practitioners to effectively build and deploy their deep learning models making TensorFlow the first choice for both theorists and engineers.

PyTorch is another popular DL framework that was released by Facebook's AI Research laboratory, and it is much preferred among researchers. Their key selling point is the flexibility of the computation graph and simplicity which makes it perfect for volatile use cases and research environments. PyTorch was introduced in 2016 and since then gained popularity because of reasons such as being easy to use, flexible, and Python-like.

Thus, relying on the dynamic computation graph, PyTorch stands out from the mentioned TensorFlow approach based on the static computation graph. An operation for constructing the graph occurs during execution in PyTorch, and hence, the programming becomes more natural and easier for debugging and constructing models. This makes it possible for researchers to try out unique architectures especially when the model architecture can change according to input data or any other factor. Second, because of the dynamism of PyTorch, its programming style is better aligned with Python's approach, meaning it is simpler to read and has fewer syntax errors.

PyTorch's compatibility with other Python libraries, including, NumPy, SciPy, and others, also contributes to the same cause. It allows users to leverage a vast number of scientific computation libraries available in Python space. Furthermore, is very compatible with the native Python debugger pdb used in improving the debugging of complex layered neural networks. PyTorch also computes on GPU thus making it fast for training and inference on high-end systems.

This that was developed by Facebook—to be largely preferred by researchers—is currently production-ready. Before TorchServe and the creation of PyTorch Lightning, the framework lacked tools to make the deployment and scaling of models for production easy. In the same way, libraries such as PyTorch Lightning hide a significant amount of the initial code and thus help in implementing and training models while paying attention to the core of the model itself.

Since its inception, the PyTorch community has expanded vigorously featuring significant contributions from academic institutions, and industries. As many new and novel research papers and state-of-the-art models are being developed in PyTorch, its usage has further surged among researchers and academia. Due to the easy-to-implement feature of the framework in terms of experimentation and trying out various prototypes, it perfectly fits the needs of many researchers involved in the development of new deep-learning approaches.

MXNet, which has been tightly developed by Apache, is another competitive deep learning framework with is highly scalable and efficient in distributed training. MXNet's flexibility and fully enriched programming model permit the developers to train as well as define deep learning models with either imperative or symbolic means and have more control of both.

In the deployment mode, MXNet uses symbolic execution, which is quite akin to TensorFlow's static computation graph to achieve the best optimization while on the other hand, it has an imperative mode which is similar to PyTorch. What this double mode does is that it brings fast experimentation during the build phase and tight optimization during the runtime phase.

MXNet has been praised for its performance, especially in large-scale distributed training. Scaletality is one of the key goals the framework was developed for; it was tested and shown to work properly on multiple GPUs and distributed architecture. It has therefore found its use in cloud computing, particularly in tasks such as training models in parallel across many machines. AWS deeply adopted MXNet as one of the available deep learning frameworks for its users who are handling extensive research projects.

It is also capable of using minimal memory which is a bonus for embedded systems and even Mobile GPUs. MXNet is also CPU optimized which makes it efficient in executions where GPUs cannot be used or are not efficient. Such characteristics make MXNet a rather flexible framework, particularly in situations, where computational capacities are reduced or large-scale implementation is required.

Within the context of the current communities and ecosystems, MXNet is still not as popular globally or for enterprises as TensorFlow or PyTorch, but it has steady growth in the contributors and user base. It encompasses numerous high-level utilization cases that include natural language processing as well as computer vision Deep learning applications and the framework integrates with distinguished deep learning libraries and tools.

 Hence, TensorFlow, PyTorch, and MXNet are all appropriate frameworks for deep learning tasks each with its strengths. TensorFlow thus comes packed with a rich ecosystem and is engineered to be deployed in production use cases, giving it an edge where high and flexible performance is desired. In particular, dynamic computation graphs and explicit control over tensors using Python increase PyTorch's popularity among the research community and those who opt for flexibility in experiments. Specifically, the modularity of MXNet, especially the distributed training and the low memory consumption, make it suitable for large-scale deep learning and environments with limited resources. With the emergence of new and smarter deep learning models, these frameworks you have outlined here will continually play a significant role in innovations of the future AI applications.

5.2 Frameworks for Embedded Systems: TensorFlow Lite, ONNX, Caffe2

Embedded systems are a crucial aspect of the current generation of computing devices, including smartphones, IoT trinkets, and future self-driving automobiles that cannot efficiently and compactly compute data on the fly and make real-time decisions without powerful hardware systems. The final set of requirements suggests that to run deep learning models on these devices the developers require specific frameworks for their form factor and operating environment. The well-known platforms to implement deep learning on the embedded system are TensorFlow Lite, ONNX (Open Neural Network Exchange), and Caffe2. All these frameworks provide unique features suitable for the effectiveness of embedded devices as far as possible, emphasizing performance to go well with efficiency.

TensorFlow Lite is one of the extensions of Google's widely used TensorFlow framework, which offers a solution for deploying machine learning models to mobile and embedded platforms. TensorFlow on the other hand is specially designed for servers and GPUs and contains large-scale computations whereas Tensorflow Lite is optimized for containing these computations and memory usage which is beneficial in smartphones, IoTs, and edge computing situations.

Another benefit of working with TensorFlow Lite is the capability to convert TensorFlow models that were developed at the large scale of the TensorFlow framework to a more compact structure more suitable for running on the devices. This conversion is performed using some practices like quantization, whereby the weights are from 32-bit floating point to 8-bit integers. This not only has the effect of reducing model size but also of accelerating inferencing, because lower precision processing reduces the required amount of computation. In addition, it is possible to have the effectiveness of the deep learning models enhanced in real-time applications with the help of hardware acceleration through delegates for the GPU and Edge TPU belonging to Google.

 TensorFlow Lite also gives developers the ability to create machine learning models that can be capable of running through different devices, be it an Android or iOS smartphone, micro-controllers, or any other embedded system. This is because TensorFlow Lite can operate offline, the models do not need to depend on the cloud decision-making process as a way of achieving results. This is particularly important in use cases where speed of computation is of essence such as in smart cameras, voice-controlled applications, and in healthcare where data privacy is paramount.

However, as TensorFlow Lite is just a part of the TensorFlow system, developers have access to a vast number of pre-trained models, tools, and libraries. However, TensorFlow Lite's Model Maker makes the fine-tuning of pre-trained models on new data even less of a concern by fully automating such tasks, thus making TensorFlow Lite appealing to developers who wish to deploy AI applications at scale without the need to train their models from scratch.

ONNX is an open-source format used as a middle database or manager between one machine learning toolkit and another. Facebook and Microsoft worked on ONNX to tackle the problem of deploying the models with different frameworks by providing a format to them. It allows for the models trained in one certain framework – PyTorch, for instance, or

TensorFlow – to be deployed in another ecosystem with little change.

Embedded systems are one area where ONNX is most useful because it makes the process of porting machine learning models for CHisplex devices more efficient. For instance, developers can save a model in PyTorch, convert it to ONNX, and then, the converted model can be loaded in a different runtime engine like ONNX Runtime or TensorRT which is, for example, suited to be run on an embedded system. This flexibility is useful in embedded systems applications where a number of the devices might use a certain runtime Environment while another requires a different one yet the same model is to be deployed.

ONNX supports many deep learning frameworks and optimizes its performance for several hardware accelerators, which is the advantage of ONNX for deploying models. For instance, ONNX Runtime which executes ONNX models can get optimizations for various devices, CPU, GPU, and others like Intel's OpenVINO and NVIDIA's TensorRT. This makes it possible for developers of the deep learning models to achieve high performance regardless of the hardware resources available which plays a crucial role in the development of the embedded systems.

The problem of invoking the ONNX models can also be solved by the fact that it enables the model deployment across different OS and programming languages. It makes it especially attractive as a solution for developers who have to work in mixed environments where embedded devices can run on varied platforms and can be programmed in various languages. The ONNX model affords a level of cross-platform model deployment which aids in its management in various complex and disparate systems.

Caffe2 is composed of Facebook's new lightweight deep learning framework and is used mainly for mobile and embedded apps. Caffe2 was developed to solve the most complex challenges of deploying models in low computing power devices such as a smartphone, an IoT device, and an autonomous system. Although Facebook has integrated Caffe2 into PyTorch, the latter still holds significant importance for specific embedded use cases because of its singular pass design and optimized performance.

Caffe2's one key advantage is that delivers deep learning performance on both CPU and GPU and that would be great for embedded devices where one would like to fit a lot of processing without too much complexity. To this end, Caffe2 features a highly optimized backend for low-power processors which is essential in the processing of real-time information necessary in embedded systems with a focus on power-saving.

As for the original Caffe2, it is used in most mobile applications where low-latency inferencing is quite essential in AR/VR apps. It became possible to include only those subroutines in the developer's code that he required, which resulted in the lowered memory consumption and the increased rate of execution. Moreover, Caffe2 embeds with the substrate of hardware accelerators such as NVIDIA's Jetson platform to enhance the efficiency of edge AI for robotics, drones, and autonomous vehicles.

Due to Caffe2 integration into PyTorch, the principles of the architecture are still affecting the current state of deep learning in embedded systems. Mobile adaptation in PyTorch now encompasses several of the enhancements and stripped-down characteristics of Caffe2 now built into PyTorch for the presumptive, effortless transfer of mobile PyTorch models.

TensorFlow Lite, ONNX, and Caffe2 are three critical frameworks through which deep learning models are executed on an embedded system. It stands out from the industrial rivals as the development tool specially fit for converting full-fledged versions of machine learning models for mobile and IoT devices while supporting hardware acceleration out of the box. ONNX plays a crucial role as an interface to transport models from one development framework to another and from one hardware environment to another. Caffe2 is an ancestor of a modern mobile-first PyTorch, which rose as the optimized model deployment in resource-constrained environments was called for with Caffe2's lightweight architecture and mobile and embedded applications background. As the power of artificial intelligence unfolds its demand into embedded systems, these frameworks will be paramount for developers intending to glow in performance, efficient consumption of resources, and the ease with which the device can be deployed. These frameworks support smart devices, IoT devices autonomous systems, or any business applications, which offer the features and benefits to implement deep learning systems in embedded devices.

5.3 Development Environments and Tools

Various tools and environments are required to support various applications as for the case of embedded systems and deep learning for doing specific works that would be suitable for the said fields. Right from creating sets of instructions for basic hardware to making IoT devices run machine learning algorithms, a developer needs an atmosphere and tools, that are easy to work with, highly scalable, and efficient. When it comes to deep learning and AI tools and environments installed on the SoC, there are always computation cost requirements, memory overhead requirements, and real-time response time requirements. Therefore choosing the right development environment helps in designing, testing, and implementing embedded systems hence such an environment has significant roles.

IDEs are among the highly used environments in the development of embedded systems and the

Integrated Development Environments (IDEs) are some of the most commonly implemented environments. An IDE or Software Development Tools are those that is used to connect the development of the code with the testing and correcting and some IDEs contain the tools. Some of the commonly used IDEs in the vertical of embedded system programming include Eclipse, Keil uVision, and Visual Studio Code. They offer certain characteristics and aspects such as syntax highlight, version control, and even h/w bug checking.

Some specific categories of developers, who are working on development for some specific hardware platforms like microcontrollers or FPGAs, like Atmel Studio or Xilinx Vivado for max. This kind of environment allows direct control of the addressed hardware, as well as basic operations like for instance debugging or firmware downloads. Additionally, prebuilt versions come with the best libraries and drivers which minimize much time when fixing the hardware projects. For instance, the Xilinx Vivado enables the designer to test the FPGA logic circuits that are incorporated into the circuits and/or devices that come with AI models that play a key role in optimizing AI-based embedded systems.

The new trend in the sphere of AI and deep learning is the emergence of machine learning development environments as it is observed. Tools like Google Colab or Jupyter Notebooks are platforms by which the developers get the opportunity to write Python code, build models, and visualize the data all in one place. However, these environments are mainly used in prototyping and training models and can be used in embedded applications mostly at the time of model emergence. For instance, the models developed using TensorFlow in the Jupyter environment can be easily migrated later to TensorFlow Lite for an embedded system. Of course, the capacity to work together with others, to think in terms of ideas, and to test these in any given live project has a tremendous amount of worth, particularly in less structured environments such as research and development.

Regarding the hardware aspect of the AI model deployment, particular settings are required; these are TensorFlow Lite, PyTorch Mobile, and Open VINO. Of all those tools, TensorFlow Lite's Model Maker plays a crucial role in creating power-efficient and performance-optimized models that will be deployed on the embedded systems. They also help to fine-tune the transferred learning of the pre-trained models on other datasets of interest; they also convert the models to TensorFlow Lite. TensorFlow Lite Converter which is the sibling of TensorFlow Lite is a tool that optimizes the model size for better execution on Raspberry Pi, Google Coral, and microcontrollers amongst others.

Another function that ONNX Runtime has is the deployment of models which is important for models in real-world applications. While ONNX as said earlier can be used to port models from one framework to another for example PyTorch to TensorFlow or from one hardware to another, it is an open-source offering. The ONNX Runtime constitutes the execution environment of these models on different hardware, from the general processors and graphics processors to the dedicated hardware, the Intel Open VINO, and the NVIDIA TensorRT. Among all the features of ONNX Runtime, it can be said that the main advantage is that the solution works best when used in limited conditions, which is the main condition for using OS in embedded systems.

The cross-compilation tools are essential in the system development from the model development to the system deployment in the development of the embedded systems. They allow programmers to write the code in the host computer and then compile and download it for running in the target embedded system possibly with a different architecture. Some of the examples of cross-compilers are GCC CMake and Make files which are used to compile binaries for a specific class of CPU such as ARM or MIPS. It becomes very important at the time of developing an embedded system as the execution capabilities of the target devices are quite low and the compiled versions of the application code cannot use heavier compilers that may be available in the local system. They ensure that compiles from high-powered workstations can be optimized as well as deployed on low-end devices.

When chasing bugs at the embedded systems level, one cannot do without Open OCD (Open On-Chip Debugger), and GDB (GNU Debugger) among others. Some of the debugger's help make the developers understand the primitive by which they can set the breakpoints, or even step through the code and observe its memory content at that particular stage. This level of control is especially useful in embedded applications and systems development because a problem, that may be residing in the hardware platform, cannot be debugged using software debuggers. Many of the above tools have JTAG interfaces, an interface commonly used for hardware debugging, and that enables an engineer to connect directly to the embedded processor.

Other development tools facilitate development and they include the Simulators and emulators. The aforementioned tools allow the developers to emulate the actual systems they developed to ascertain the performance of the said systems on a physical hardware platform. For instance, QEMU an acronym for Quick Emulator enables the emulation of many hardware architectures and its main use is the emulation of hardware in what are known as Embedded systems well before an actual tangibility of the same is made. In the same manner, Proteusis was significantly used in the development of the embedded system to simulate the microcontrollers and their peripherals to test the program to run on real hardware without having to use the system.

Such platforms can be applied for the continuous integration and delivery process in the context of embedded systems to remove any actions in the process of code building and testing for future deployment. These tools are integrated with version control programs such as Gith which means that, when different developers are evolving the different parts of the same project or system, the modifications made by any person go through the revision control system to iOS and validate before the updated code is incorporated in the final system enctype= []. CI/CD pipelines are already more important in embedded systems, but they are even more so in the case of integrated embedded systems indicating that the number of integrated developers also increases in the process.

Analysis and optimization are key in enhancing the performance of the technical features in embedded systems. Tools like 'and' are used to profile code, what matters include space, time, and CPU cycle. In resource-hungry applications such as AI, where speed of inference and utilization of the underlying hardware is even more important there are more specific profiling tools such as NVIDIA's and Intel's that tell a lot about how models run on the hardware, be it GPU, CPU or even ASICs. These tools help in analyzing the performance by locating the bottlenecks and in optimizing both hardware and software aspects of the SoCs about the strict standards of power and performance demanded by the embedded systems.

The evolution of most systems with special emphasis on systems containing AI and deep learning requires a variety of tools and platforms that are best suited to the characteristics of the embedded hardware platforms. These systems are key to ensuring effectiveness and reliability and for this, IDEs, machine learning environments, cross-compilation tools, debuggers, simulators, and profiling tools. As the sophistication of this kind of system increases over time mainly due to the incorporation of significant Artificial Intelligence tools, the selection of the right tool and development environment plays a central role in current and future implementation and deployment.

5.4 Deployment Pipelines

If such applications like embedded systems or any products need them then deep learning models can be employed there.

Before going deeper into the analysis, it is important to understand that an effective software deployment environment has to be equipped with a clear and productive working framework that is called the deployment pipeline. A deployment pipeline can be described as a set of actions that take an application or a model from the developers' environment to the production one carrying out a set of tests and tuning procedures about the given constraints and characteristics of the target environment. Specifically for embedded systems, the bottlenecks are memory, processing power, and energy which makes the pipeline deployment even valued. Deployment is to enable the model to run optimally on the intended device, be modified, and run efficiently with minimal power consumption.

In most of the cases of embedded systems, the sequential steps for the software deployment process are: Based on the above analysis of the existing trends in the field of software deployment it is possible to define the following general steps, which may be used in further implementation of the software deployment process in different cases: The stages of model development include the model training and testing which is one of the initial stages exercised in the process. In this stage, the machine learning models are developed, fine-tuned, and validated with Class Big Data at high computing or in a cloud environment. At this stage, TensorFlow,

PyTool, and MXTool are used for constructing and training the deep-learning models. The model is often judged on its accuracy, and, maybe, its clarity, its practicality, and other skills for it to perform as planned on the offered task. However, this stage takes place in what can be calibrated commodity hardware like GPU or TPU, which is not similar to the restraints of the supposed embedded context.

The fourth sub-process is the optimization and conversion process after the model has been trained and tested in the use of the pipeline. This step is necessary because the hardware on which the model is to be deployed is much less resilient than the development hardware. This phase consists of a method or technique applied to reduce and scale down the data model and its energy and memory needed to function. A rather common strategy is model quantization which requires the conversion of the model's weights and activations from 32-bit floating point numbers to 16- or 8-bit integers.

However, the reduction of the model size also came with the advantage of reducing the time taken to make an inference which is vital in the case of real-time embedded systems.

Apart from quantization, there are other optimizations used which include; Pruning: when those neurons or parameters are pruned off which are insignificant or of no relevance. ; and Weight sharing: where the weights are placed in clusters to reduce the similarity as much as possible. Such optimizations are usually done using tools offered by some frameworks such as TensorFlow Lite/ PyTorch Mobile which has tools concerning the conversion and optimization of models for mobile and embedded uses. After this optimization, the converted model is transformed into another format to be used in the target device hardware architecture for instance TensorFlow Lite Flat buffer format or ONNX Runtime Format.

When the designed model is ready the pipeline moves to the testing phase which is done in a synthetic environment. Once the model is built, it can be used to go to the hardware directly but, it is important to determine the performance of the model within the simulation platform. It is in this step that the developers get a chance to witness things like; overflows in memory, new performance breakthroughs, and even compatibility problems. In this stage, there is the utilization of pre-existing simulators such as QEMU or platform-specific coupled Raspberry Pi, NVIDIA Jetson, or Google Coral. These tools imitate the behavior of the embedded device whereas for the real implementation here in the illustration as observed by the developers they are giving or showing how the developed model operates under some restricted environment before using the physical devices.

For successful testing in a simulated platform, there is a step in integration with the software of the embedded system. Most embedded systems run some form of real-time operating system or a tiny Linux and the model must be blended into the other code in the application that processes data, controls sensors, and manages the user interface. At this level, the developers put down the drivers, Application Programming Interfaces, and other system-related codes in a bid to create an interface between the developed AI model and other sub-systems in the embedded system. For instance, in the case of self-driving cars, the model needs to communicate with the vehicle's control system to avail the data captured by the LiDARs and cameras and to alter the car's speed or direction.

Adaptive testing or CI/CD methods are gradually becoming integrated into many embedded AI systems as well as other more repetitive application-oriented industries such as automotive, robotics, and IoT. CI/CD pipelines also eliminate situations where developers modify new code or models and do not use them for testing for hours, or even days and then deploy them. This often involves the conducting of what is known as 'integration tests' on both, the emulated environment as well as the concrete physical components, on which the embedded software is installed. Continuous integration tools such as Jenkins, Travis CI, or GitLab CI are the most commonly used ones for running tests and deploying code. For an embedded systems CI/CD there has to be processes that update the firmware or models in the board and then test and evaluate the board. What this means is that when the changes for the system are being implemented then these updates do not introduce new faults or worse performance.

After integration and testing are done at the CI/CD pipeline level, the next process is model deployment on the physical device containing the device embedded. In this stage, the selected and integrated model is used in implementing the target device. This can be done manually or through the use of computer computer-automated system depending on the stage of advance of the deploying system. In most of the cases, the model is pushed through the Over-the-Air (OTA) update mechanism mainly in the IoT devices, autonomous systems, remote sensors, etc. OTA updates allow developers to bring in a new model or a system update to the device that is already out in the field. This is especially so where multiple devices are located from different geographical domains as in smart farming or industrial conditions.

Once the model is deployed on the device, the functions of monitoring as well as providing feedback are major components of the pipeline. It is equally important after deploying the system to keep track of the system's performance to ascertain whether the intended model is working as expected in actual practice. Some of the data that is gathered by monitoring tools include system performance, energy used, model updates, or system failures and abnormal incidences. As has been already mentioned, in countless embedded systems, it is critical to perform real-time monitoring and logging, which is paramount in particular application domains such as healthcare or autonomous driving. This is because any problems or declines in performance should be identified as soon as possible to apply updates or patches to avoid system problems.

Apart from monitoring which occurs in real-time, there could be a section of the pipeline, for example, where model updates and the retraining process take place. It must however be noted that as new data is captured especially in highly evolving areas, then the model may require new training or fine-tuning. It also allows the model to modify the application to suit changed conditions or more new kinds of input. For example, in self-driving cars, over time as more data on driving is obtained, models used in car learning can be updated to address new driving environments, types of roads, or weather among others. Retrained models can then be pushed back to the devices through the CI/CD pipeline The CI/CD pipeline in the given approach entails the following Merchandise Inspection.

Last but not least a deployment pipeline should be tight and secure. In most cases, embedded systems are networks or directly connected to the internet, and therefore the security issue is very crucial. Models and system software files must be protected from copying and unauthorized access during the process of their transmission. Such implementations as secure bootloaders, cryptographic signatures, or utilizing a security module in the devices' hardware to ensure the initial flawless state of the software and the corresponding models have been maintained.

AI models need to be deployed in the embedded systems and this has to occur through a proper and effective deployment process. The pipeline starts with the model, followed by optimization of that model, and then testing in a simulation environment, in addition to testing in the actual hardware environment, interfacing of this software with the embedded software, and finally downloading of this software onto the actual device. The current feedback and constant updates guarantee that the system will be very effective throughout its life cycle, and it will also be secure. Thus, with the increase in the role of embedded AI across various industries, the issue of having proper deployment pipelines will emerge as an essential factor to consider for these systems.

5.5 Model Conversion and Optimization

Taking into consideration those factors that are conducive to deep learning models in embedded systems, one of the most important factors to consider is model conversion and optimization. Such steps help to make sure that a model, which normally requires high calculation capacity such as GPUs or cloud computers, can run on small-scale embedded devices. These computations, if carried out in usual computing environments have a much higher memory, computation power, and energy than what embedded systems have. Hence, model conversion and optimization is a critical task to fill the gap between model development and its deployment so that the models should be able to execute and perform optimally in such resource-scarce devices.

In most cases, conversion of the base model forms the initial process in the development of telematics functions. All deep learning models are primarily built with high-level systems such as TensorFlow, PyTorch, or MXNet. These frameworks offer great mechanisms for training and testing models but the models resulting from these frameworks as raw

entities are highly bulky and complex requiring/".
$+/ for embedded systems. Conversion tools then
convert these models to formats that are more
friendly to the embedded system's hardware
architecture and its performance capabilities.

For instance, there is the TensorFlow Lite which is a
framework for deploying TensorFlow models in
mobile as well as an embedded environment. It
allows developers to build models from the usual
TensorFlow ones to the small models for real-time
deployment to such platforms as smartphones,
Raspberry Pi, or microcontrollers. The conversion is
highlighted by resizing the model and omitting
unused elements allowing TensorFlow Lite for low-
latency, energy-efficient inference. Likewise, ONNX
(Open Neural Network Exchange) offers a method
that is independent of the framework which
converts a model that has been built in frameworks
such as PyTorch and TensorFlow among others into

a format that can be optimized and deployed across various hardware platforms.

The other area of model conversion is the ability to practice precision reduction this is a process of reducing the numerical precision of model parameters and activations. Deep learning models in most cases work in 32-bit floating point precision, they give highly accurate results but are very resource-hungry in terms of computing power and memory resources. Nonetheless, the embedded systems take advantage of the lower precision data such as 16-bit or even 8-bit integers. Another frequently applied method of precision reduction is called quantization: it decreases the size of a model by replacing floating-point weights with fixed-point integers. This might cause a minor decrease in the accuracy of the model, but the gains in memory optimization and power consumption make it perfect to be deployed to hardware, especially embedded systems. For instance, quantized models are very efficient when they are run on specific platforms such as Google Coral's Edge TPU, this is because Edge TPU has been designed to optimize 8-bit computations.

Another powerful methodology is pruning Apart from quantization, the following methodology is also widely used. Removal of some of the parameters in the neural network can be achieved through pruning this reduces the unnecessary areas that are not useful when making the predictions. In their development process, there are some neurons and connections in deep learning models that are useless. Pruning defines and eliminates them as part of the redundant components that need not occupy valuable space and resources in a model while performing approximately the same tasks whereby the efficiency of the model is improved. This is specifically beneficial where the amount of memory and processing power is limited, which is quite common in the case of many embedded systems. For instance, in the convolutional neural networks, CNNs applied to image recognition problems the pruning can get rid of numerous filters in the convolutionary layers but this does not bay affect the precision of the model significantly.

After that, the converted and optimized model should be ready to use and then pass through the next step in the pipeline which is calibration of the model for the target hardware. The reason why calibration is necessary is that it tries to optimize the model on the hardware it will be running on. For instance, the behavior of a model when running on a desktop GPU will be entirely different from when it is run on an NVIDIA Jetson or a microcontroller that will have significantly fewer computational capabilities. Such tools as TensorRT from NVIDIA reduce deep learning computational overheads through architecture awareness of the GPU, layer swapping, and layer fusion, respectively. This process makes sure that the model is as efficient as possible for the hardware setup while meeting the performance requirement.

Weight sharing is also another major optimization strategy and it entails combining weights that are similar to maximize the storage efficiency of a model. This technique operates when the person discovers groups of weights that are in the neural network and are of similar values whereby, they can be made to take the same value. Thus, weight sharing also decreases the number of unique weights which have to be stored as well thus leading to a general model size compression. It is most helpful where models are running on platforms with a very limited number of memory resources like microcontrollers or low-power IoT devices where every kilobyte of memory can make a very big difference.

Optimizing a model to deploy it in an embedded system would not be complete without the use of Edge computing and hardware acceleration. The major difference of edge computing is that computation and analysis do not happen on a remote server, but are located near the data source and eliminate latency and high bandwidth usage. In this regard, the models executing on embedded devices are usually improved by utilizing hardware accelerators such as TPUs (Tensor Processing Units), NPUs (Neural Processing Units), and FPGAs (Field-Programmable Gate Arrays). These accelerators are precisely developed to help in the high computation necessary in deep learning to enhance the models' performance. Because of these optimizations, some of which include parallel processing and particular memory handling, accelerators are capable of running models in real time, which is critical in use cases like autonomous driving or real-time video processing.

It is often as well the case in model optimization where inference time is also a focal point of reduction so that it can meet real-time processing.

As mentioned above, the real-time response might be critical to controlling processes or machinery in an embedded system in applications like in medical devices or drones. There are several ways to decrease the amount of inference time, it means less depth of a model, or using such networks as MobileNets or SqueezeNet which were developed for usage in the conditions of limited resources. These architectures are balanced and less complex to achieve reasonable accuracy but have less computation load.

Last but not least, a similar method used for optimizing the models is batching which can also enhance the models used in the embedded systems. Batching adapts in such a way that all inputs can be passed through a neural network in one step while in actuality, individual passes are made on the inputs. The ability of the system to process data in sets is useful since the system can then combine the sets and take advantage of parallelism to do its work.

However, in applications that occur in real-time where the response time is important the batch size should be small or even possibly one at a time.

Reconstruction of the model and model improvement is crucial to facilitate the application of deep learning models in embedded systems where the resources are scarce and the performance standards are highly demanding. Tools such as TensorFlow Lite, and ONNX are transferring tools that transform high-level models to formats suitable for embedded implementation while techniques such as quantization, pruning, and weight sharing minimize the computational and memory intensity of the models. Special calibration for certain hardware and applying accelerators including TPUs or FPGAs helps to optimize performance. With the increasing use of embedded AI, learning these techniques will be vital for developers who wish to implement intelligent models in real-life applications in a limited-resource environment.

CHAPTER 6: DESIGN AND OPTIMIZATION OF DEEP LEARNING MODELS

6.1 Model Design Principles

When it comes to developing machine learning models especially the deep learning ones for embedded systems, there are certain design principles that one has to make sure that the created model follows. These model design principles not only define the process of designing the model but also play roles associated with the use of the models. These principles are important for building accurate and resource-efficient models irrespective of how large AI models one may be working on if one is developing a new optimized model for constrained hardware like an embedded system.

It does not matter whether these models are going to be used one day for making decisions or not, modularity remains one of the most important principles when it comes to designing models. A modular model is constructed from more elementary components which are easier to be modified or substituted. This principle enables changes and expansion in the model design process hence adopting a robust design. For instance, a convolutional neural network (CNN) may be regarded as a set of sub-layers where every sub-layer has its specific functions such as feature extraction and dimensionality reduction. These layers can be individually altered, tuned, or swapped making it easier for developers to test out several configurations when working at the architectural level without having to come up with a brand-new model. To my mind, modular design proves advantageous when applied to the domain of embedded systems, as such systems are often built with an array of computational constraints: to transition from a heavy component to its lightweight version, the model has to be modular.

The use of simple design can also be said to be an important design principle in the design of the microcontroller. It is revealed that adding more layers and parameters to the model will increase the accuracy rate. Still, some drawbacks of this technique are high computational complexity, large memory consumption, and high power consumption. In real-world application scenarios many times the task is to design the simplest architecture that can achieve the necessary performance. Popular models such as MobileNets, EfficientNet, and more have been developed with the main aim of balancing the accuracy and device usage possible on various platforms such as Mobile and embedded. In this way, through simplicity, developers can construct models that require less time for execution than optimization while being more interpretable and easier to maintain.

Regarding simplicity, the principle of minimalism always presupposes the absence of any unnecessary complexity in the model. This can be done by culling or regularization by eliminating a layer or neuron that is not helpful in the training of the model or by eradicating the features that are not contributing to the model's efficiency. The same can be said about the data used to train the model; they also have to be minimalistic to some extent. Thus, by a wise choice of possible attributes and features that possess high predictive value, the number of model inputs can be minimized along with the training time and computational demands for inference. The most important for securing minimum design is to always remove unnecessary parts of the code because memory and processing power are scarce on embedded systems.

The optimization of the target environment is also one of the vital principles in model design, especially for embedded applications. A model, that is optimized to work with a high-performance server system, may not be very efficient with an embedded system device. Hence, one needs to take into consideration the limitations of the target environment right from the design phase. This entails consideration of characteristics such as processing capability, memory size, and the power consumption of devices where the model is to be deployed. Methods such as quantization, or when the number of decimal points in the model's weights and activations is reduced, or pruning where unneeded neurons are stripped, are employed to ensure that models run optimally on low-power devices including microcontrollers or edge computing.

Another important principle is scalability Scalability of any project is a key principle that has to be kept into account in the process of creating an information system. Although the emphasis may be twofold on defining a model for a given application or data set, models must be scalable and built with scalability in mind. It also means that as the model is fed with a larger data set or the problem formulated requires more sophistication, it should be possible to add onto the model without having to train it all over again or redesign it. More specifically in deep learning models for example through transfer learning and fine-tuning, the models can be easily reused for new tasks. These techniques are most effectively used in applications such as embedded systems where availability of training data may be a challenge, and where constraints on re-training could be tight. In transfer learning the models are initially trained for a similar set of problems and then are further fine-tuned for specific tasks thereby reducing time and effort in deployment.

The other principle of model design is robustness. The high variability has to work on a reliable model that will not degrade even if the data is full of noise or missing some parts of it. It is particularly crucial in real-world scenarios whereby data may be noisy and unreliable, for example, in the context of smart environments, self-driving vehicles, or wearable health monitoring systems. There are ways of making it less fragile such as data augmentation, which is where training data is modified to mimic variations that would be observed in reality or there are ways of making the model less dependent on the training data by way of regularizations. Product-oriented systems, especially the ones that are modeled to be operational in physically changing surroundings, need to be highly abstracted from the external environment to guarantee optimum performance consistently.

The principle of generalization also applies to model design as it does to the construction of a program. It means that a good model should be able to classify the new data points that it hasn't seen during the training to some extent at least, instead of doing well only on the training data set. To get good generalization one has to focus on the training process and pay attention to the type of the validation and testing dataset, regularization, and overfitting. In other circumstances where the model is going to be used in different and dynamic environments, for instance, voice recognition systems, or medical diagnosis models based on data from different patient populations, the ability to generalize is critical to the continued success of the model.

The last principle is flexibility which has also been a recent addition mainly because of the current trends in edge computing and AI-enabled IoT devices. It has to allow for flexibility which is coverage, change in data, different inputs, and even the change in platforms it runs on. This flexibility is normally realized in methods such as online learning, whereby the model's parameters are updated during normal usage. Since a considerable number of devices are located in remote areas or are built into places that are difficult to access, flexibility is essential to extend the model's lifespan and utility for the embedded systems.

Efficiency is one of the most important factors to be taken into account when designing models in embedded systems. Most of the embedded devices are run by batteries and therefore the energy should be conserved or used sparingly. Developing efficient models therefore requires that not only the software that makes up the model but also the hardware to which the model is run is considered. Some of the methods used in reducing energy consumption include weight compression, using less power precision arithmetic, and applying early exit techniques in which the model is capable of exiting the processing earlier when the result is highly probable. Furthermore, TPUs and NPUs are the hardware accelerators for carrying out ML models with low power consumption which makes them so crucial in power-sensitive systems.

Last but not least, there is the basic principle of explainability, which is more and more applied in model design. There is increasing use of AI models in various sensitive areas such as; medicine, and banking among others and therefore every decision made by an AI model should be explainable. This is particularly apparent with deep learning models as they are considered black boxes, or at least a great part of it. Conceptualization of models with explainability entails utilizing inherent architectures, such as decision trees or focused types of attention to structure the aspects of records such models use, as well as using fundamental techniques such as LIME or SHAP after the model has been generated. The decisions made in a model could be safety critical in some applications and since the models can perform computations in real-time, it becomes essential to prove to the users as well as the regulatory authorities that such decisions can be explained.

When constructing models in machine learning, several principles precede the top level, which guarantees that apart from being precise, models constructed are efficient, flexible, and extendable. Starting with modularity and simplicity, up to robustness, scalability, and energy efficiency, these principles govern how the models are to be structured and implemented across the various application domains, but especially in those that are most constrained in terms of resources such as embedded systems. Thus, if developers follow these design principles, they will be able to design models that may fit with the real-life application requirements given the environment constraints.

6.2 Transfer Learning and Fine-Tuning

Transfer learning coupled with fine-tuning is now an irreplaceable tool in current advanced deep learning technologies, especially when using limited data or computing power to solve enormous problems. That is the reason why these methods enable the developers how to use ready-made pre-trained models, to minimize the time and effort to create highly accurate and effective models from scratch. The phenomena of transfer learning and fine-tuning are becoming a foundation in AI and deep learning progress to make profound intelligence more transportable and applicable in different areas and apply the CIS devices.

In other words, Transfer Learning refers to a practice in which a model trained on one task applies the knowledge that it has gained in that task to another related task. In deep learning, one fine example is ImageNet for image classification, the machine is trained with a large amount of data from which, it needs to learn features that are shared or common features in different tasks such as edges, shape, and texture. Instead of the process of training a new model which is a time-consuming as well as data-intensive process, developers use a pre-trained model and adapt it for a new task such as identifying diseases in X-ray images or objects in a robotic system.

Transfer learning can be enhanced by the inability to work with more data unlike when one is learning from scratch. Training deep learning models from scratch often entails the utilization of massive labeled datasets, which frequently are scarce in certain application areas such as healthcare, cyber security, or industrial IoT. This way, the developers can start with generalized knowledge, which already has been acquired by the model, and having less amount of data can increase its performance much better with the help of fine-tuning. This is especially so in real life since organizing data collection is expensive, complicated, or sometimes even impossible.

Transfer learning is generally employed by transferring the initial layers of the given model since these layers analyze more general characteristics and probably update the subsequent layers which analyze certain characteristics in more depth to the new domain or retraining these layers with regards to the requirements of the new domain. For instance, in a CNN example using ImageNet, the initial layers may complete feature extraction of edges and corners of objects while the last layers boast the identification of various shapes and features of the objects. If we are applying transfer learning with a different image classification problem say identifying certain animals where most of the features will be the same, only the last layers are trained to identify the new categories. This makes it greatly beneficial for models since only a portion of the model parameters need to be updated, hence saving computation power and time.

As has been shown here, transfer learning is not limited to image classification only. It also applies in natural language processing NLP where models such as BERT and GPT have transformed the way different language models are trained and implemented. They are initialized with such huge text data sets so that they learn syntax, grammar, dependencies, and contexts between words. Using such small task-specific datasets, developers can then fine-tune these models for specific NLP tasks among them being sentiment analysis, machine translation, and chatbots. This approach has made a new generation of NLP models available for domains even in specialized fields in which extensive language data sets may not be available.

Another important issue about transfer learning is that it has been mainly applied to imitated environments like embedded systems. Training deep learning models from scratch is computationally intensive and this is often expensive to perform on Raspberry Pi, microcontrollers, or edge hardware. This is addressed by transfer learning which enables the developers to employ the already trained models which have been trained on the powerful cloud servers or GPUs. However, for fine-tuned and optimized applications in an embedded system environment, these models may be trained and used. This makes it possible to perform computations on devices with less computational power and memory, and without the need for the cloud for inference constantly.

One example of this is mobile nets which can be regarded as a family of models that is specifically tailored for the use in mobile and embedded vision applications. These models are light and compact and perfect for use in devices that require less computational power such as edge devices. Using transfer learning, developers can adjust the pre-trained model of Microsoft MobileNet that was trained in ImageNet, for example, for such operations as face recognition or object detection on the smartphone and IoT device. It can be seen that the fine-tuned model can obtain high accuracy while keeping a low computational overhead necessary for real-time inference in embedded devices.

The second technique, known as fine-tuning, is a must-do step and complements transfer learning. Fine-tuning entails training for a selected pre-trained model for some or all of its parameters on a new set of data. Therefore, the extent of fine-tuning is proportional to the amount of similarity between the primary task for which a given model was trained and the new one. If the tasks are very similar, for example, if the next task implies the recognition of various types of dogs after training on a general image classification, one may need to fine-tune only the last layers. Thus, if the new task is relatively significantly different, e.g., from image classification to medical image segmentation, several layers could be retrained.

Due to the effective use of the fine-tuning technique, models can be made to be resilient to the special needs of a specific task. For example, a semantic segmentation model may require different regions of an image than a simple person detection model. This way the pre-trained model will adapt itself and focus on the key features important for the new task that it will perform better than if it had to be trained from scratch. Another area where Fine-tuning can be applied is when models are needed in different environment or condition. Specifically, in the case of autonomous driving, the pre-trained model fine-tuned for sunny and clear conditions can be fine-tuned for foggy or nighttime conditions thus making the autonomous driving system robust.

What's more, fine-tuning is also a cheaper method even for smaller organizations and individuals who cannot afford to train large models right from the start. You might need weeks, even months or years, big data, and the latest and the greatest 'heart and soul' hardware to train a deep learning model from scratch GPT or ResNet. Fine-tuning, on the other hand, is seemingly a much more lightweight operation and can usually be performed even with substantially less computational resources, on 'standard' GPUs or even CPUs. This makes it possible for researchers, startups, and developers to use advanced deep learning techniques in their problems hence expanding the AI development across the board.

However, certain issues affect fine-tuning in its effective execution. Some of them include overfitting, whereby the model identifies insignificant breaks, thus producing high-frequency values with low volatility. If the new dataset is either relatively small or not diverse enough, the fine-tuned model can get 'locked in' to the peculiarities of the new data and will generalize poorly to new and unseen instances. To this, measures such as data augmentation, dropout, and early stopping can be used during the fine-tuning regime. They allow preserving the general knowledge learned during pre-training from getting 'forgotten' and following the fine-tuning dataset specifics too strictly.

However, the decision on which layers have to be fine-tuned again is a critical factor to be considered. In transfer learning it is typical to make or set the initial layers of a given model, where higher semantic features are usually less relevant, and unalterable – a set called freeze. Nevertheless, at some point, only the necessary layers may be fine-tuned, while in other cases, especially when the new task is quite different from the initial task, it is better to fine-tune more layers or even the whole model. This depends on the amount of similarity of the tasks and the computational power that will be used for the retraining process.

Transfer learning and fine-tuning are valuable techniques that have revolutionized the methods of using deep learning models. With the help of pre-trained models, developers thus can avoid the need to gather large amounts of data and use a lot of computational power, which means they can utilize state-of-the-art artificial intelligence in a variety of tasks from image classification to prose parsing. Whether training a model, fine-tuning a MobileNet to fit an embedded system, or re-purposing a language model for specialized tasks, these strategies greatly lower the deep learning development's entry barrier and enable widespread use throughout numerous sectors.

6.3 Quantization and Pruning

The two primary methods used in the optimization of the deep learning models are Quantization and Pruning which mainly come into play when the models' implementation is on resource-limited gadgets like embedded systems, mobile devices, and edge computing. These methods are concerned with finding ways of keeping the size of the model compact, enhancing the speed of inference, and at the same time keeping power consumption low while at the same time keeping the accuracies at a reasonable level. Hence, quantization and pruning are some of the popular approaches popularized in today's world of advanced AI applications in healthcare, self-driving cars, and smart gadgets.

In its simplest terms, quantization is a process of lowering the accuracy of the numerical values involved in a neural network; weights as well as activations. The majority of deep learning models, in general, can be trained with 32-bit floating point numbers which is also referred to as single precision. Although such a level of detail can be beneficial during training, it can be detrimental during inference as the applications are executed on devices with less computational power. To this end, quantization is exercised in the current work by transforming the model's weights and activations to representations with a limited floating point precision, <FP16 or 8-bit Integer,> or INT8. This reduces the precision of the model and as a result, has a smaller size, takes less time for computation and consumption of memory resources which are all essentials to an embedded system.

This is often the first reason we hear people trying to justify their use of quantization because it reduces the amount of memory needed. Because lower-precision data types need less number of bits to encode every number, quantized models can considerably decrease memory size. For instance, changing a model from floating points to integer 8 halves the memory size and can be almost four times smaller as one example. This is especially true in the case of smaller deeply embedded devices that have to meet stringent size constraints that include one Megabyte of ROM and RAM for both the kernel and the applications. Through the concept of quantization, large models can now be deployed in microcontrollers or mobile platforms as the optimization is not much of a loss to modeling prowess.

Besides memory savings, which have been described in detail in this work, quantization has another advantage – it speeds up computations. As we observe, smaller precisions consume less time on the computation and therefore result in faster inferences. This kind of speedup is especially useful when working with applications that require live audio or video such as webcasting, voice recognition, or online auto-navigating. Current acceleration hardware like GPU, TPU, NPU, etc, are built to cater to low-precision computations thus providing support for INT8 and FP16. This introduced quantization of the model which when implemented empowers the developers to harness these hardware accelerators to the optimum without the need for extra hardware.

But as will be seen, quantization is not without its problems. It must be pointed out that one of the most significant trade-offs of training models on such subsets is reduced model accuracy. Such representations are necessarily less accurate compared to these FP32 counterparts and small numerical errors get compounded during inference. This can lead to a decrease in performance which can be significant – especially for applications where the accuracy is of high value such as diagnosis from medical images or investing strategies. To counteract this, a process called quantization-aware training (QAT) is applied most of the time. In QAT, quantization is done in silico during the training phase such that the model will be accustomed to working with lower precision than that of full precision. This allowed the model to generalize on quantization and thus when the model was finally quantized, the loss in accuracy was negligible.

That is why, another technique to reduce the accuracy loss is post-training quantization (PTQ). In PTQ, the model is introduced to float precision and then, quantized after the completion of the training phase. This is easier and quicker compared to the QAT but accuracy will be affected; this majorly impacts models that require precision for operations. However, PTQ is an efficient technique especially when the models used are in devices with low memory and power such as IoT sensors or Edge AI devices where its trade of accuracy and efficiency is reasonable.

Whereas in quantization the method is applied in an attempt to minimize the quantities being used in a model, in pruning it is done in an attempt to minimize the coefficients of the model. Pruning operates in a way that involves determining the weights or neurons which do not significantly affect the result of the neural network and then removing them, or the layer in which the neurons are located. Such "non-significant" parameters are thresholds that, as a rule, are close to zero or the coefficients for which a change affects the loss function to a negligible extent. In other words, pruning necessitates the omission of such parameters, which results in streamlining the model regarding computation as well as memory.

Perhaps one of the most familiar types of pruning is weight pruning which involves zeroing out or setting certain weights in the network to zero thus eliminating them from the network. This leads to the construction of a hyped weight matrix which in turn is easier to store and perform computations with. The next approach is structural pruning where the neurons or even the filters, or even the layers of the network, we eliminate them. Structured pruning is more beneficial from the hardware perspective because it results in a higher reduction in the computational requirement and is easier to implement on a hardware accelerator.

Pruning is most effective when used for model compression. Sometimes, models such as CNNs or RNNs are trained with excess parameters that could lead to really large models. Thus, if several developing parameters become excessive and some of them can be thought of as unimportant or less significant, the model's size may be greatly diminished without increasing the level of error significantly. Such compression is useful when deploying the models on devices with less storage space or where speed and time of inference are especially important.

Another disadvantage of pruning is that performing this is not an easy task because it is complex to determine the correct balance between the rate of compression and the rate of accurate estimation. When many parameters are pruned out, some of them may be invaluable to the model, and hence, a big drop in the performance will be noticed. Hence, the pruning is usually done in stages, wherein only a small percentage of the parameters are pruned in every iteration after which the model is refined to regain the accuracy that was affected. This process of repetition enables the model to fine-tune itself with the limited architecture in a way that the results will still be promising even though the number of parameters available to it is few.

Pruning is also often associated with model spareness is also a very closely related notion. This is why a pruned model is also known as a sparse model since most of its weights are zeroes and make no impact on the model's result. Sparse models require less memory and time in comparison with dense models while they are more compatible with specific types of hardware devices including the specialized matrix multiplying units. At times, pruning results in models that are not only quantized but also ones that have faster inference, since sparse models can choose to exclude computations during the application phase.

When quantization is combined with pruning, the advantages that are reaped are even more significant. This means that modern developers can fine-tune their models to be more precise than traditional machine learning while using fewer parameters and numbers altogether which also makes for very efficient to be deployed in embedded systems or the like. Together these two benefits enable the modelers to achieve tremendous compression of model size as well as shortening of inference time all this without much compromise to the accuracy of the predictions. For instance, models utilized in self-driving or autonomous aerial vehicles, smart appliances, or health self-monitoring devices could leverage both approaches to execute complex AI computations on low-energy ICs.

These two are very efficient approaches to deep learning model optimization especially with issues to do with computation constraints, memory, and power. These techniques help the developers to design models with less accuracy, fewer parameters, and in turn less size, speed, and energy without much sacrifice. Thus, quantization and pruning are going to remain the essential topics as AI transitions to edge devices and embedded systems making powerful machine learning more practical for a wide spectrum of applications ranging from self-driving cars to smart IoT gadgets.

6.4 Knowledge Distillation

It is thus seen that Kd is an informative model compression approach that occupies a significant place in enabling deep learning models to be much more optimized and appropriate for use in constrained devices including the embedded systems, cloud-based and mobile applications, and edge nodes of computer networks. In other words, knowledge distillation is the process whereby the knowledge contained in a big and intricate teacher model is transferred to a more manageable student model. The objective is to allow the student model to replicate the performance of the teacher model despite having much fewer parameters and computational power than the latter. This process is especially helpful in situations where it is impossible or unadvisable to launch big, compute- and power-hungry models.

Knowledge distillation was originated by Hinton et al.; since then, the concept has found use in various research areas and real-world applications. Some of the drivers of the development of knowledge distillation include; there has been an enhancement in the complexity of the deep learning models recently. Such models as GPT-4, BERT, and ResNet could contain billions of parameters making them very accurate but sequentially slow and requiring a lot of memory. These models generally entail high computational needs for inference in terms of GPUs or distinct hardware, hence, they are not very useful for real-time applications or implementations in edge devices such as smartphones. Knowledge distillation provides a solution to this dilemma by enabling developers to compress these models while keeping most of the performance; thereby extending the use of Artificial Intelligence in different fields.

The core process of knowledge distillation involves three main components: module four includes the teacher model, the student model, and the soft targets that are generated by the teacher model. While training the student model, what the student model does is not rely on the ground truth labels available in the dataset but opts to learn from the soft targets produced by the teacher model. It turns out that these soft targets are rich in the information about the relationship between different classes and as such the student model is provided with more subtle forms of guidance than when employing the hard labels. For instance, while the hard label might just be the correct class (e.g.. "cat"), the soft targets from the teacher model might be 80% confident that the image is a cat, 10% that it is a fox, and 5% that it is a dog. Such distribution of probabilities corresponds to the learned information the teacher model has and aids the student model to generalize better.

Knowledge distillation also has the advantage of knowledge distillation enable the student model to obtain not only the final output of the teacher model but also the partial representations of intermediate data learned by the teacher model. They retain high-level information and structures that otherwise the student model learning might be significantly impeded by if it has fewer parameters or lower model complexity. The strengths of these representations can then be used to capture the behavior of the teacher model and enable the student model to perform to its level of proficiency more efficiently in terms of memory and computation.

Training the student model through knowledge distillation typically involves minimizing a loss function that combines two components: It consists of the traditional cross-entropy loss concerning the ground truth labels and knowledge distillation loss concerning soft labels generated by the teacher model. The distillation loss is multiplicative with a separate parameter called the temperature. This temperature parameter defines how 'smoothed' is the soft target distribution that is outputted by the teacher model. The effect of higher temperature is that the probability distribution is more smooth as the differences between the predicted probabilities for each class are lesser. This is advantageous for the student model as it will grasp more detailed information concerning the relation of different classes and therefore generalization is enhanced.

Knowledge distillation is known to have several other benefits besides enhancing the efficiency of the model such as; One of the most important is its capability to help in deploying models on edge devices and embedded systems. In use cases which include self-driving automobiles, industrial robots, and wearable healthcare check devices, computational and power resources are constrained and hence cannot support the utilization of large models that demand great power. In the same way that a large teacher model is divided into a student model, these developers can therefore deploy great AI solutions on these devices without significant loss of performance. Although it is smaller, lighter, and faster, as presented in the previous section, the student model can still provide real-time inference, which is important for fast-based applications such as gesture recognition, object detection, or speech synthesis.

Another crucial advantage of knowledge distillation is the aspect of model explainability as well as the model's resilience. A similar problem with extensive models is that they are superimposed as black boxes, thus users, and in many cases, developers do not know for sure how the models arrive at certain predictions. Applying the knowledge in the form of a smaller student model has fewer layers in its structure as compared to the consolidated knowledge system and therefore the student model analysis can be less complex and more comprehensible. This can be especially valuable in sensitive domains such as healthcare or finance where it is of paramount importance to know the ins and outs of the model. Besides, the original study highlighted that knowledge distillation enhances the models' resistance to adversarial attacks. The student model, after training with more detailed and encompassing soft targets origin from the teacher model, can better handle noisy or noisy data because of the resistance that it has.

Knowledge distillation is also very versatile and can be combined with virtually any architecture and applied to a large variety of tasks. For example in natural language processing specific large pre-trained models like BERT and GPT are widely used and knowledge distillation has been applied to distill models such as DistilBERT which performs nearly as well as BERT but is trained with fewer parameters and faster inference time. Similarly in computer vision, in the aforementioned manner, knowledge distillation has been used for building compact neural networks for image classification, object detection, as well as, semantic segmentation. Such flexibility allows knowledge distillation to be a versatile approach for improving deep learning models in several domains and tertiary applications.

In addition to the original ways of knowledge distillation with standard teacher-student relations, there have appeared more complex forms of the technique as time went by. Self-distillation is one such technique where the model used is as the teacher or the trainer and as the student at the same time. In this case, the model extracts its knowledge using the trick of learning from intermediate representations and sequentially improving on the predictions during the training steps. The presented approach of self-distillation does not require an external teacher model, which results in enhanced model performance and increased model robustness so that it can be recommended for use for optimizing deep learning models in conditions of a limited number of available sources.

Another modification is multi-teacher distillation in which several teacher models are applied to train one student model. This approach enables the student model to get knowledge from knowledge sources through different teacher models knowledge depending on the input it produces, which potentially increases the student model's generalization across a larger set of tasks. For example, given a multi-modal AI system where both image and text inputs are processed, two teacher models could be trained using images and text respectively; the resultant knowledge learned from both the teacher models could be integrated and compiled into a solitary student model which outperforms in both the modalities.

That being the case, while applying knowledge distillation has its benefits, it also has some drawbacks. By far, one of the most difficult tasks is choosing the type of teacher model to be adopted. An ill-trained or overtrained teacher model does not give good soft targets for a student, thus, degrading its performance. In the same regard, knowledge distillation also helps in compressing models but with the trade-off of the model size and accuracy. As is the case with most compression methods, achieving the optimal rate of compression and computational efficiency is a matter of adjusting several hyperparameters, including the temperature and the weighting factor of the distillation loss.

Knowledge distillation as a general idea is a rather useful and effective practice for optimizing deep models and ensuring their functionality for the targeted platform. This is the art of transferring knowledge from huge and complicated teacher models to much lighter student models to get fast and accurate systems. Regardless of its application in CV, NLP, and other fields, knowledge distillation is indeed a very strategic asset in the journey to achieving greater scalability of AI. Thus, with the development of AI to embedded systems, mobile devices, as well as edge computing, knowledge distillation will surely continue to be a significant enabler of AI's advancement.

6.5 Hardware-Aware Neural Architecture Search (NAS)

Hardware-aware NAS can be considered one of the groundbreaking trends in artificial intelligence, which is aimed at optimizing neural network architectures not only from the accuracy point of view but from the viewpoint of their performance on concrete hardware platforms. While deep learning models are becoming larger with millions, if not, billions of parameters, their architecture and sizes have made it challenging to implement them on devices with limited resources which include smartphones, the Internet of Things, Voice assistance, and other edge devices. Other conventional approaches used in designing ANN may comprise a reference to the performances such as accuracy or tasks without considering the constraints and possibilities of the target platform. Hardware-Aware NAS fills this void by taking into account in the preliminary design phase the limitations of the underlying hardware platform to arrive in the end with a model that delivers both high accuracy levels and efficiency.

Therefore, the main concept of NAS stands for Neural Architecture Search which is a process of automating the design of neural networks. Instead of choosing the architecture of a model by hand: how many layers to put, what kind of operations, and how big filters are NAS employs search algorithms to go through the vast space of possible architectures and find out which architectures are the best for the given task. It is usually approximated using reinforcement learning, evolutionary algorithms, or gradient-based optimization methods to efficiently search through architecture space. NAS has also been used in the discovery of highly effective architectures such as EfficientNet, which belongs to Google and NASNet.

However, one of the drawbacks of traditional NAS is that it is commonly optimized based solely on accuracy enhancement or task optimization neglecting the fact that the final model will be run on some specific hardware. This can lead to architectures that are when accurate, yet too large or too demanding on the computation resources, which is particularly important in the case of edge devices, mobile platforms, and other contexts with limited computational resources. Hardware-aware NAS is an extension to the standard NAS process; where the objective that guides the search process encompasses hardware considerations including latency, memory usage, power usage, and computational expense. The aim is kept simple, namely identifying architectures that are both accurate and efficient enough for practical use across a diverse stock of hardware.

Still, by making the whole architecture hardware-aware, NAS helps address an important problem – an inextricable link between accuracy and efficiency. The complexity of a neural network increases with depth or the number of parameters used in the model and these additions can often enhance the efficiency of the network but at the same time require many computations which may not be efficient. On the other hand, by down-scaling the architecture, it is effective in cutting down computational costs but this is likely to lead to a very poor accuracy. Hardware-aware NAS helps developers handle this trade-off more efficiently due to the model implemented that defines the strengths and weaknesses of the hardware. This way, it can choose architectures that provide the highest potential performance for the given amount of available hardware resources and thus guarantee that the model does not demand too many resources of the target device, while still providing a high level of performance out of it.

EfficientNet which is a family of CNN developed by Google using NAS that operates both on efficiency and accuracy is another example of hardware-aware NAS. Another advantage of EfficientNet models is that these models are scalable this is because one can scale the depth, width, and resolution of the EfficientNet model to implement it on different hardware. This makes them very flexible, and usable for deployment in a huge category of devices including high-end graphic processing units in data centers and mobile central processing units in smartphones. It is possible by building NAS with consideration of specific hardware requirements as in EfficientNet to gain higher accuracy in image classification tasks in comparison with previous architectures, such as ResNet or Inception but with less usage of resources.

Another example of the use of hardware-aware NAS worth mentioning is the creation of models for edge computing and IoT devices. Such devices often have low computational capabilities, memory, and energy constraints; it is not practical to implement large Deep Learning models. Hardware-aware NAS allows for designing models for neural networks that, although can be carried out on such devices, are highly optimized for these platforms and provide accurate predictions. The consequence is wide-reaching in the potential of using AI for various technological advancements including real-time object detection in drones, voice recognition in smart speakers, and anomaly detection in machines for industries.

Another constraint of hardware-aware NAS is latency which is considered to be amongst the most significant metrics for this type of NAS. Throughput is the rate at which the model processes inputs and generates responses and its relation to latency in real-time applications such as autonomous driving augmented reality, and video streaming. In such cases, any time delay in inference is costly, and hence, the need to optimize neural networks in terms of latency. Hardware-aware NAS integrates the latency constraint into the search process so that the actual architecture requires real-time performance in the target application. This is very crucial with the current trend of moving intelligence to the edge where models need to run on edge devices that are constrained in terms of computational power.

Energy utilization is yet another factor to be considered in hardware-aware NAS, especially in battery-limited devices like mobile phones, smart wearables, and IoT sensors. Real-time running and training of convolutional and recurrent models often demand extensive computational resources, and operating these holographically on a device can be power-hungry. Because modern hardware has many constraints and shortages of energy, hardware-aware NAS can optimize architectures by focusing on the selection of operations and layers that consume less energy. Specifically, compared to expensive operations such as standalone convolutions, the hardware-focused NAS prefers cheaper operations like depthwise separable convolutions to design less energy-intensive models of high accuracy.

Memory footprint is another factor that is considered in hardware-aware NAS. Memory constraints are even more so applicable to scenarios such as embedded systems and edge computing devices that are often constrained with little RAM or storage. Described large models with numerous millions of parameters may be challenging to deploy on such devices at all, let alone make inference reasonably fast or at least possible. Hardware-aware NAS alleviates this with solutions that directly aim at architectures' memory consumption by eliminating superfluous layers, decreasing the feature maps' sizes, or compressing weights. This makes it possible for developers to implement high-performance AI models on these devices with limited memory while not significantly compromising the models' effectiveness.

This means that while hardware-aware NAS does depend on the existence of effective accurate models of the target hardware's performance, their effectiveness has been proven. These models aim to predict the number of operations and memory and energy requirements of potential architectures during the NAS phase. The search algorithm can use the fact that the target emulator allows the simulation of how a particular architecture will perform on the target hardware to make conscious decisions as to which architectures should be considered in the next step of the search process. The main difficulty when creating accurate models of the hardware execution is the necessity to obtain precise information about the particular hardware and algorithms employed by the neural network. However, with the regularly occurring new types of accelerators, including GPUs, TPUs, NPUs, and others, researchers have started to pay more attention to constructing more accurate and efficient models for hardware performance prediction of NAS.

I point out that the effect of hardware-aware NAS is not only for edge devices and embedded systems but can be generalized. This situation is especially apparent in data centers that are the default place for running large models on GPUs and TPUs, there is a strong demand for efficiency. Unsurprisingly, some of the workloads have increased in scale over the years, and cutting power consumption and increasing computational efficiency become a matter of cost. Hardware-aware NAS has useful applications in making data centers deploy better models for use in AI systems with no need to purchase new hardware, therefore lowering power consumption in the process.

Concerned NAS is considered a revolutionary step in the way of optimizing AI models via hardware awareness. In particular, the incorporation of hardware factors ranging from latency through energy consumption to memory footprint into the architecture search process allows for the deployment of accurate and efficient enough neural networks on all kinds of devices ranging from small edge IoT sensors to powerful GPUs. With the development trend of applying AI applications in various fields, the deployment of hardware-aware NAS to support the better AI model deployment to practical application scenarios will be more and more significant to make AI more open, large-scale, and sustainable.

6.6 Case Studies and Practical Examples

Educational aspects and real-life examples play a significant role in the elaboration and assessment of the technologies including deep learning, generative AI, and embedded systems. Presenting examples of how these theories are applied, modified, and fine-tuned in practice, they outline definite strategies on how certain problem situations might be addressed. Looking at several case studies, we can study the development of artificial intelligence and embedded systems across several industries, healthcare, the automotive industry, manufacturing, and consumer electronics. These issues are going to be discussed further in the context of several outstanding case studies to understand their practical applicability and issues related to the implementation of AI systems in modern conditions.

Such strategies may include the application of Artificial Intelligence in the diagnosis of diseases and medical imaging. The use of deep learning models especially the convolutional neural networks (CNNs) has been very crucial in enhancing diagnostic models in the health sector. One of the most familiar applications is the use of AI algorithms to diagnose diseases including cancer through scans. The use of Mammography for breast cancer detection together with Google Health working with hospitals to use artificial intelligence models in identifying the diseases also increases the strengths of this approach. In this case, a model of deep learning psychiatry was trained with ten thousand labeled medical images and learned to diagnose cancerous tissues with accuracy levels as high or higher than human radiologists. This case study will give you an idea of how AI could enhance the functionalities of physicians, decrease the chances of wrong diagnoses, and help accelerate the detection of deadly diseases. But it also reveals problems: data protection issues, the data quality issue, and the AI system implementation in clinical practices.

Another such example is the application of embedded systems and artificial intelligence in self-driving cars. Tesla Motors, Waymo, and Uber are some of the companies that have reached the forefront when it comes to autonomous vehicles that are mostly required to make decisions in real-time. Sitting at the core of this technology is what you may well know as neural networks, or deep learning which interprets data gathered from various sensors including LiDAR, radar, and cameras affixed to the vehicle. These models include object recognition, lane maintenance, object evasion, and navigation. Tesla's Autopilot system, for example, helps drivers in functions such as driving on highways or even parking using neural networks and sensors among others. One of the specific difficulties in this domain is the fact that the models should be able to operate with a low latency because delays can lead to accidents. Here, forward-compatible and hardware-aware NAS is employed in the process to fine-tune the models for real-time implementation on specialized hardware platforms such as NVIDIA's Drive platform. This case should remind safety-critical designers of how important model efficiency and effectively utilizing hardware are.

In addition within industrial automation, the employment of artificial intelligence as well as embedded systems is changing the whole of manufacturing. One good example is the implementation of predictive maintenance where AI algorithms are trained with the data obtained from sensors attached to the industrial apparatuses to estimate when the machines are most probably to develop faults. Companies such as Siemens have deployed AI-based predictive maintenance solutions which lower on time and boost the productivity of the production processes. By analyzing recurrent features in signals coming from sensors, including vibrations and temperatures, AI-based forerunner machines can estimate potential failures, which suggests that maintenance can be done ahead of time. This helps not only to prevent the number of repairs during operations from being high but also the useful life of the equipment is prolonged. However, using such systems in factories is much more challenging than in other environments; noisy sensors, interaction of AI with industrial systems, and exposure to severe conditions that might hamper the reliability of the predictions.

Smart home devices are commonplace across the globe perhaps this is why the two most tangible innovations in AI and embedded systems find their most realistic use in consumer electronics. Today's AI-enabled connected home appliances including Google Nest, Amazon's Alexa, and Apple's HomeKit have become indispensable parts of human life. Each of these devices employs an AI algorithm for activities such as voice recognition, voice synthesis, and recommendation. For example, NLP models in Amazon's Alexa allow users to manage smart devices in the home, set alarms, or listen to music. A major concern in this application is matching the use of the AI models with low-power solutions yet the models' performance has to be very high. Because these devices are constrained by limited hardware and should not hang for too long, engineers apply methods such as model quantization and pruning that allow the models to be made smaller and the computations performed on them to be less demanding while still achieving nearly the same results. These devices are good reflections of how Artificial Intelligence can easily be incorporated into tools that are useful to individuals daily and make life easier for them.

Another engaging example is generative applied in the entertainment sector. There are also many different generation models including GANs and

VAEs, which are used to produce realistic images, music, or videos. DALL·E, created by OpenAI is a representative of generative AI that can generate unique images on the textual descriptions. Along the same line and in a more professional manner, GANs have been applied by the movie industry to produce effects, images of characters or even to 'youthify' actors. An interesting example that has been common in the recent past is the process of altering the appearance of actors or characters in the scenes using AI to make the actors look young again as it was done in the movie "The Irishman. " These models produce high resolution of the surface and facial expressions which enables them to blend with the final video. However, besides the tremendous possibilities of its application in most creative industries, the problems of the authors' rights and attributions of the contents, deepfakes, and possible abuses remain huge issues to be discussed.

The efficiency of AI is also being valued in the financial sector in such areas as fraud detection and algorithmic trading Deep learning models have been integrated by banks and other types of financial institutions for conducting analyses of users' multiple transactions to identify fraud signs. These models are set to detect outliers in real-time with the specific goal of alerting the authorities of suspicious transactions. For instance, while using applications, Mastercard uses artificial intelligence algorithms that analyze billions of transactions going on per day to flag any fraud, in real-time or nearly real-time. Likewise, algorithmic trading firms employ artificial intelligence models to study the financial markets to make trading decisions in a very short time. These systems comprise highly complex neural networks whereby market information, news feeds as well as other data feeds are analyzed to predict the probable changes in price and then generate buy and sell orders on their own. However, such models may generate huge profits, at the same time creating problems of market instability and questionable ethical standards of super-fast, AI-based trading algorithms that take advantage of minor discrepancies in stock prices that a human trader could not hope to accomplish.

Finally, it is important to note that research on climate change is an emerging field of artificial intelligence. The applications of the embedded systems which have AI capabilities are used for environmental monitoring, weather forecasting, and air pollution measurements. For instance, Machine learning models are employed to interpret satellite images to check on deforestation, or predict the occurrence of wildfires, or determine climatic change effects on ecosystems. Today's giants such as IBM and Google are developing AI systems to enable organizations to manage environmental risks. An example of this is **Google's AI for Earth** where the giant uses machine learning to find out information regarding the quality of water, the habitat of species, and changes in the use of land through satellite images. Applying AI in these applications is not easy because a large amount of data is involved and there is a requirement to process a large amount of data in real-time while at the same time, the model should be reliable and very accurate.

These cases and use cases demonstrate how AI and embedded systems can unlock change and value across sectors. Who knew that AI would be used in sectors such as healthcare and self-driving automobiles to entertainment and climate research? However, these application areas also present key issues such as data privacy, hardware limitations, ethical issues, and highly reliable and real-time required performance. Thus, by analyzing these cases we can get closer to the real-life application of AI and the outcomes that can be expected due to that, which allows us to create a basis for further advancement of the technology.

CHAPTER 7: IMPLEMENTATION OF GENERATIVE AI MODELS

7.1 Generative Adversarial Networks (GANs)

GANs are among the developments considered to mark some of the most groundbreaking advancements identified within Artificial Intelligence. GANs for the first time introduced by Ian Goodfellow and his co-authors in 2014 have changed the way models are designed to generate new data in AI. Different from the prior work of classification or regression, GANs are intended to generate new, or "generate" data, such as image, video, or audio data. This ability has paved the way for several opportunities in every field such as entertainment and gaming, health care, finance, and more.

At the core of a GAN is a unique architecture composed of two neural networks: that is, the generator and the discriminator. These two networks are designed in an antagonistic structure so that both are engaged in zero-sum competition. The generator aims to generate data that is indistinguishable from normal data in the sense that the discriminator cannot distinguish between real and fake data. On the other hand, the discriminator's role is to differentiate between the actual data that had been fed in the training data set and the fake data that has been produced by the generator. In the long run, as this process is iteratively taken, both the generator and the discriminator are enhanced— where the generator will be generating better data that are close to real while the discriminator will be enhanced to better identify fake data generated by the generator.

This opposition is what makes GANs so strong and versatile; it is the primary reason behind their strengths. In a way, the generator and discriminator continuously challenge each other to achieve state-of-art results, where GANs are capable of generating outputs that are similar to the genuine outputs in most cases. For instance, as regards image generation, GANs are capable of generating realistic high-quality images that depict faces, landscapes, or objects that are real or imaginary. Such capability has made the GANs useful in the creative arts such as graphic designing, computer games, and even in movie making.

Perhaps the best-known example of GANs at work is the generation of deep-fakes hyper-realistic fake videos where the face of a person can be inserted into another person's body or an entirely new video can be synthesized based on real footage of another person. While deepfakes raised concerns about ethical issues regarding the manipulative use of AI, it is a good representation of the potential and capability of GANs in reproducing realistic data. These are the same techniques that can be used for more harmless applications like enhancing the graphics of a video game, creating new virtual characters for films, or when the real data sources are limited to train an AI model.

Another application of GANs can be in transforming the creative field of art and design where art can be generated through combining the creativity of an artist with the capabilities of Artificial Intelligence. It is applied by artists and designers who want to create different images, paintings, and sculptures, which cannot be created with traditional methods. Using GANs, certain artists upload several styles and techniques and then let the generator develop its version. The outcomes can sometimes be astonishing and encouraging, giving a feeling of how the collaboration with artificial intelligence may look from the theoretical side in the future. In fashion, GANs have been applied to the creation of new colors and patterns of clothes and the creation of virtual models that can be used in the simulation of new styles and designs, boosting the creativity and number of attempts in the fashion industry.

In addition to the creative industries, GANs are also revolutionizing the scientific community, especially in the areas of health. For instance, in medical imaging applications, GANs have been used to improve the quality of the scans, reconstruct the missing values, or synthesize new medical images that could be used for training other AI models. In one case when collecting data with real clinical data is challenging due to privacy constraints or the rarity of cases, the use of GAN to emulate the real data is useful. For example, GANs have been utilized in generating synthetic fMRI images that allow for developing AI-based methods for detecting brain tumors, or in modeling those clinical situations that are rather limited in the available datasets.

Now, in the field of finance, various fields of usage of GANs are investigating how they can be used, for example, to generate synthetic financial data to check different algorithms or to identify fraudulent transactions. Through presenting a range of realistic scenarios in the market, the GANs can be used to educate models in an organization's financial industry to perform in response to existing or emerging economic conditions or are capable of revealing features that might not be discernable with other conventional methods of analysis. However, the application of GANs in finance has also caused concern since the same technique used by the enhanced model can be used to fabricate and falsify different financial reports or even manipulate genuine data for snakes' aims. The fact that the cyber technology of GANs has such a double-edged use, where the same tool can be used for the benefit of both parties as well as for harm against the other party makes it an interesting object of ethical considerations.

That is why the process of training GANs can be very tricky, especially, when it comes to the balance of generator and discriminator. If the discriminator overpowers the generator for a long time, it may end up generating poor learning results and something referred to as the mode collapse in which the generator only generates a limited variety of inputs. On the other hand, if the generator gets too powerful, the discriminator will be outcompeted and hence, the generated data will not improve much. To have such a balanced decision on its hyperparameters is crucial to make both networks develop and improve in periods by applying new training algorithms.

However, there are always new variants of GAN getting proposed in the literature for bettering the stability and performance of GANs. For instance, there are Wasserstein GANs (WGANs) which were meant to solve issues of instability that are common with initial GANs since they employ a more stable loss function for training. Likewise, there are styles in StyleGANs Word for users to have better control over the style and structure of images they want to generate rather than using attributes like color, texture, and form. These advancements have expanded the capability of the GANs model and increased its potential usage and applicability to other tasks and cases.

Another great advancement in the designing of GANs is the application of this model in unsupervised learning and semi-supervised learning. In the past, GANs needed an impressive array of samples that have been tagged to help the discriminator and this may pose a major challenge to acquire. However, this has been disapproved in recent developments since it has been revealed that GANs can be trained with less labeled samples, thanks to the synthetic nature of the generator. This makes it possible to train AI models in various fields in which obtaining labeled data is a challenge time-consuming and/or expensive.

However, the loose coupling trend of modularity is observed as of now GANs are used as standalone and integrated into other AI models to form advanced systems. First of all, GANs are combined with reinforcement learning to create environments for training self-driving agents and can also be combined with CNNs for improving image analysis tasks. This possibility of combining GANs with other models shows that these models are very applicable in enhancing many applications of AI.

GANs have become one of the most revolutionary techniques in the application of AI, offering new opportunities for such spheres as entertainment and design, healthcare, and finance. The features here mean that photorealistic renders can create new possibilities for art and entertainment, research and development, and business and marketing.

However, as with any great power, there are also great responsibilities and the more recent breakthrough of GANs raises several ethical questions, especially in fields such as deepfakes and data manipulation. With the development of GANs, it is possible to speak about the enormous potential of the application of these models in the further development of AI and in forming the future society, which is full of opportunities and challenges.

7.2 Variational Autoencoders (VAEs)

VAEs stands for Variational Autoencoders, which is another class of generative models that have garnered much interest over the recent past, thanks to the techniques employed in their generation and the outcomes of samples from these models that are usually generated in the form of data reconstructions. Derived from the autoencoders VAEs effectively implement the concepts of probabilistic modeling as well as artificial neural networks to create an influential model to understand the data distribution. Whereas the autoencoder is a method that is based on the compression of the information into the space with fewer dimensions and then its reproduction, the VAEs add the stochastic component into this process. This randomness makes the VAEs capable of coming up with rather realistic data samples in a purely stochastic manner, which can be quite difficult to adapt VAEs for a plethora of applications, be it generating images from data or detecting anomalies.

In the middle of a VAE is the concept of the learning of a probability distribution over the data. Contrary to what is normally seen in an autoencoder where the primary aim is to encode the input data into a lower dimensional space such that the data can be reconstructed. The encoder network accomplishes this compression and the decoder network reconstructs the data from the latent representation. This is in contrast to VAEs that disseminate a probability density of distributions of the latent space for the input data. This distribution is usually modeled as a Gaussian, and the encoder outputs two key parameters: that is, the values of the mean, and the variance of the proposed Gaussian distribution. The decoder goes further and takes a random sample from the distribution to reconstruct the input data.

The difference between VAEs from autoencoders is that the latter employs probabilistic modeling. Instead of sampling from the data space, which contains the actual data samples, VAEs sample from a distribution that has been learned in the latent space, and then map the samples through the decoder. This generative aspect of VAEs is probably one of the most defining features of using the model. For instance, in analyzing image data; after the VAE has grasped the probability distribution of the training images it can produce images that look like the training data but are unique and are not reproductions of the originals. This makes VAEs especially useful where the generation of new data is needed for example in design, image synthesis, or in data augmentation.

The training process of a VAE involves two main objectives: rewriting the input data and also guaranteeing that the learned latent space is distributed according to some distribution, usually normal distribution. Both these goals are accomplished via a loss function that incorporates the reconstruction loss along with the Kullback-Leibler (KL) divergence. The reconstruction loss specifies how well the decoder can reconstruct the input data from the latent representation while the KL divergence term checks whether the learned density distribution over the latent space is close to the desired prior density distribution typically standard Gaussian. This regularization imposed by the KL divergence prevents the feature map from collapsing into any value and allows the feature map to be used for meaningful data generation.

A main feature of the VAE is that it can navigate between two sample points in latent space as shown in the figure below. This is the case since the latent space is continuous and organized, thus it can be easily interpolated to vary between different points which represent the various samples of data. For instance, if two points in the latent space are two different images then passing intermediate points between these two points will give a sequence of images gradually moving from the first image to the second one. This property of VAEs makes them useful for applications such as image morphing and style transfer where movement from one point in the data distribution to the other is continuous.

VAEs have also been employed in other fields for data construction and other novelty detection. Because VAEs learn a compressed representation of the data, they are capable of reconstructing the input data while at the same time, excluding noise and other unnecessary features. This makes them handy in applications like image de-noising where one desires to get a clean version of an image that had been polluted. Further, because VAEs learn the probability distribution function of the training data and therefore the model can identify anomalies; those points which do not fall within the emergent distribution of training data points. In the case of anomaly detection, the VAE attempts to reconstruct an input and if the error on the reconstruction is high then possibly the input is an outlier or anomalous.

In the creative applications scenario, VAEs have been an essential tool for the generation of items such as music, images, or texts. For instance, in dealing with music the VAE can be trained on the musical sequences and after that produce new pieces of music based on the values in the latent space. Similarly in image synthesis, VAEs have been used to generate new images of different styles or create an image from the features of two or more images. These creative applications show that there is much that VAEs can do as generative models that can create different and distinct results.

However, the VAEs have several weaknesses that are associated with them in some way. One of the possible issues is how to gain the right balance between the quality of the reconstruction and the continuity of the latent space. The KL divergence term in the loss function helps the latent space to have standard Gaussian distribution but this regularization occurs that reconstruction loss also increases. Regularization carried out excessively may affect the performances of the VAE and result in poor reconstructions of the input data as indicated by blurred or distorted images. Maximizing the reconstruction loss and minimizing the KL divergence is the major concern when training VAEs and the tuning of hyperparameters for achieving this often remains challenging.

The third disadvantage of VAEs is that VAEs may create images with less clarity or definition in comparison with images generated by other types of generative models, for instance, GANs. The models which are specifically intended to generate realistic data through an adversarial process, usually outperform in image generation tasks, and their perceived quality of images is, visually appealing. Nevertheless, it is in terms of interpretability and stability that VAEs provide the benefits. This makes control in the generative process easier, especially with VAEs as opposed to GANs which are notorious for training instabilities and lack of understanding of the underlying data distribution.

To overcome some of these limitations, scholars have put forward several modifications and enhancements to the primary VAE model. For example, there exists the β-VAE variant that adds the hyperparameter β that regulates the influence of the term KL divergence for better control of the balance between reconstructive capability and constraint of the latent space. A conditional variant of the VAE is called Conditional VAE (CVAE), where extra information is provided to the model for further use, for example, class labels or attributes. This makes it possible for the CVAE to generate data that falls under certain categories or styles, which gives a lot of control as compared to normal data generation.

Variational Autoencoders are a rich and versatile generative model with the ability to train and implement deep neural networks for encoding probability distributions. The main contribution of VAEs is the incorporation of randomness into the encoding and decoding process that makes it possible to perform image generation, data interpolation as well as data reconstruction. Despite these VAEs having some shortcomings in terms of quality than other generative models like GANs, yet, due to their well-organized latent space and flexibility, they can be extremely beneficial in many domains including art and creativity, and scientific analysis. Due to the style of generative modeling, the VAEs are going to be a significant part of the AI tools as far as the synergy of data generation, data reconstruction, and data interpretability is concerned.

7.3 Recurrent Generative Models

Recurrent Generative Models are a class of generative models where we use a Recurrent Neural Network (RNN) to generate sequential data. These models are especially suitable for tasks that involve sequential or temporal data like time-series forecasting and music generation as well as natural language processing. The integration of generative features of the neural networks with the use of the recurrent architecture in modeling has made the

Recurrent generative models one of the most formidable models for developing and modeling sequences.

The recurrent generative models are centered on the use of RNNs which are created to process sequences as they comprise a hidden state that is recurrent over time. RNNs possess feedforward connections different from other normal feedforward neural networks whereby the networks have recurrent connections enabling them to store information regarding preceding inputs. Due to this characteristic, RNNs are especially useful for inputs of sequences since they are capable of keeping track of temporal dependencies and the patterns they reveal. In the generator model of generative modeling, RNNs are used for sequence generation where each element of the sequence is predicted based on the hidden state and previously generated steps.

Today, one of the most well-known applications of recurrent generative models is in natural language processing (NLP) where they are used as text generators of coherent and contextually relevant outputs. In this model, the RNN produces a single word or character at a time and adjusts an observed hidden state on each generation. One of the prior states is used to remember past inputs and the distributions, which also lets the model produce macro-contextually consistent outputs in longer sequences while staying syntactically intact. AD L

For example in the case of an RNN-based language model, the first step is to feed the model data in the form of a large corpus of text data and in the second step, the data is used to generate new syntactically correct and semantically meaningful strings of text ranging from words, sentence, paragraph or even text passages that are stylistically similar to the data fed into the model.

Text generation using RNN-based models is more often a probabilistic approach in which, the next possible tokens of words or characters are predicted with the help of their probability density function based on the present hidden state as well as the formerly generated tokens. While training the model aims at the log-likelihood of the following token in the sequence, thus, gradually learning to generate more realistic sequences. After training the model can produce a new sequence by taking a random sample from the probability distributive learned in the previous step. This form of sampling adds some measure of randomness and thus the model can come up with new sequences when sampling but is a major downfall in terms of sequence coherence, especially over long sequences.

Besides text generation, the recurrent generative models have been applied in other areas such as music generation and time series forecasting. For instance, in music composition, RNNs are applied for the creation of a sequence of notes or chords which results in a complete musical phrase. This is possible because the recurrent architecture can relate one note with another and consequently produce music that will emulate the structure of the training data. There are some enhanced models like LSTM and GRU which are more appropriate for this kind of task because they consider long-term dependency which is essential in music composition anticipating patterns of motifs in different time frames.

Another domain where recurrent generative models work efficiently is dealing with time series data, the data in sequence format that were recorded at time points. The use of time series is applicable in areas such as stock markets weather prediction or even monitoring data from the sensors. In these applications, the output of the model is on what is the next value in the sequence, and the training is done in such a way that it captures the temporal patterns and trends in the data that are fed into it. Thus, trained the model, it can fit a generation of synthetic time-series data applicable for simulation, anomaly detection, and data augmentation.

Nonetheless, several issues are encountered in recurrent generative models, though they are active in many domains. There are several of them; however, one of the most crucial issues is the problem of training RNNs, especially for long sequences. The more elements are in the sequence, the RNNs have what is known as vanishing or exploding gradients issue when the gradients the model has to learn for weight update during the training are too small or too large. This may not allow the model to accurately capture long-term dependencies which poses a severe problem in tasks where the ability to realize proximities of distant items in the sequence determines the overall accomplishment of the task. Some of these approaches are the use of gradient clipping to control the size of the gradients to a reasonable limit and the use of more complex structures such as LSTMs and GRUs among others and despite the attempt to reduce such issues, training deep RNNs still poses a challenge.

There are two main issues with recurrent generative models which include fluctuations in the generation process as well as uncontrollable generation of output results. Unlike certain other generative models for instance VAEs or GANs, which have latent codes that can be adjusted to give a particular output, recurrent generative models use the hidden state of the RNN which is normally not as easy to control. This makes a priori control of the generation process with a view of achieving a set goal or of making sure that a given constraint is met a very hard task. For instance, in text generation, it can be difficult to control the generated text's tone or length or its style as a function of its architecture or the way it was trained.

To overcome these drawbacks, several variants and extensions of recurrent generative models have been used by the researchers. One of the extensions is the application of the attention mechanism that allows the particular model to pay attention to some parts of the input sequence when producing the new data. In NLP tasks the attention mechanisms have generally been useful in that the model is allowed to focus some of the words it has seen in the sentence for the current generation of the new iteration. This has led to the creation of other complex models like the Transformer architecture that has no restraints to the self-attention to capture information about all elements in a sequence at the same time dispelling recurrence.

Besides, the attention mechanisms, the use of hybrid models that incorporate RNNs with other types of neural networks has also been considered. For example, some of the models are hybrids of CNN and RNN since they provide the best of both worlds when working with data such as video sequences that have both spatial and temporal attributes. In these models, the CNN helps to detect the spatial features inherent in each frame of the video and converts it into the corresponding temporal features using an RNN, which makes it possible to generate a realistic video sequence, Frame-wise fused features are then fed into the decoder convolutional layer, which produces the initial video frames so that the subsequent video frames can be generated through the RNN.

Recurrent generative models are also used in the framework of unsupervised learning which consists of finding patterns in the data without providing a target value. For this reason, simply the model is made to produce sequences that resemble the training data even though the structure of the data is unknown. This is particularly beneficial in situations where the training data is hard to come by or very costly to get such as in medical research or a physical simulation. With the understanding of data patterns, recurrent generative models create synthetic data which can be further trained with other learning models, or used to understand the particular data patterns and relationships.

There are more, so-called recurrent generative models which have shown to be an essentially valuable approach to generate sequential data in numerous application fields. Some of its most important uses are due to its skills at capturing long-term dependencies and generating coherent sequences for applications such as natural language processing, music, and series temporal prediction. However, the difficulties in the training of RNNs and the control of the generation process inspire further research and developments in the field. As stated earlier, with the new architecture like the attention mechanism and the hybrid models, recurrent generative models will continue to play a significant role in the generative modeling technique and present an enormous optimistic prospect for the future of AI and machine learning.

7.4 Diffusion Models

It has been thought that generative models are among the most important topics studied in recent years and therefore another powerful model has been trained as a dialogue for the generative model called diffusion models. In terms of diffusion occurring from a physical perspective, these models are most efficient in the modeling of digital generation of data, as the result of noise gradually being 'polished' into decipherable patterns. To begin with, it is worthwhile to note that the primary strength of diffusion models is in terms of the variety and realism of samples which makes these models very helpful to supplement a set of generation methods for researchers and practitioners.

In diffusion models, the strategy behind them is mainly the iterative process of reconstruction of a sample from the distribution of the noise to the target data distribution. This process emulates the diffusion process whereby in repeated time intervals particles spread themselves all over space. However in the context of generative modeling, this very concept is developed further to create a new generative process in which noise is incrementally added to data. The diffusion model consists of two primary phases: The first one refers to a forward diffusion process, and the second one is referred to as a reverse denoising process.

The forward diffusion process is the process that makes use of the addition of noise at every step most importantly the amount of noise is gradually increased to the test noise until the final distribution yields nearly the test noise. It is done deliberately with a view of making it incremental and progressive so that there can be a realization of having to grow from data to noise. Small noise is introduced with every step in the forward process and therefore the transition into noise is smooth and realistic. This forward process can be defined as a set of transitions that move forward to a particular noisy version of the data.

On the other hand, the reverse denoising process aims at trying to backward diffuse through the forward diffusion process to filter out noise from the noisy sample and get back the data. In this process, we utilized the neural network which is learned for predicting and estimating the noise that has been added in the forward progressive stage. Hence, the neural network requires learning about the reverse transition probabilities to make a sample denoised and of good quality. During training the generated samples are post-processed back to their clean state in a bid to make the models as realistic as possible through iterations.

Probably, the main advantage which can be attributed to the diffusion models is that they can ensure that the generated samples are high-quality and at the same time, possess a highly diversified range of variances. Different from other generative models that often have some weaknesses, for example, mode collapse where the synthesized samples are not very diverse, diffusion models are designed to work for any distribution of data. Due to the fact the diffusion process is conducted gradually, the model allows for assessing the tangible characteristics as well as fine distinctions between each sample of the data, eventually giving an account for the number and variety of realistic samples created. That is why the diffusion models are best suited to perform the tasks that require the generation of high-quality images, sound, or any other output data.

The models of diffusion have been highly effective in some real-world deployments of the technology. Some of these methods, for example in image generation, the Diffusion Models have brought about the generation of high-resolution pictures with detailed features and textural aspects. This gradual process of refining facilitates the virtue of discerning even the finest of details and structures thus creating images of the specimen that closely resemble actual real samples. Further, in audio synthesis, the use of diffusion models has been informative when synthesizing different samples of sounds that are realistic to capture the small details such as the timbre and pitch variations of quality audio.

Unlike the traditional generation models, the diffusion models can control the generation process with the help of a noise schedule. Just as the noise schedule determines how noise is added and removed throughout diffusion, a schedule can be more or less precise, elaborate, or complex. The noise schedule therefore makes it possible to have more control over the generative process hence the effect of the noise schedule can be compared to sample quality and diversity. Because of this flexibility, the diffusion models can perform most tasks with different data types as the need arises.

Like any other models of diffusion, the diffusion models too have issues or challenges that the users normally experience often in the course of applying the models. One of the major challenges is the computational aspect that comes with the training of these models as well as obtaining samples from there. The diffusion process implies several steps; the last of which presents the neural network with computations to be done. This can turn out to be very time-consuming computationally, particularly when dealing with large data sets or if the models involved are large or complicated. Authors also did a lot to try and improve the efficiency of the diffusion models for example, by doing numerous modifications of the training or by trying to reduce the number of steps in the sampling.

The other problem that still causes some confusion in arriving at the most suitable noise schedule is the determination of the optimal settings for a given job. Various amounts of noise can greatly affect both the quality and the diversity of the synthesized samples and more often, tuning to the correct noise schedule takes time. This may take a lot of time and researchers are still in the process of developing ways and means of incorporating methods that could assist in determining suitable noise schedules within a short time though this is still in its development stage.

In addition, the cost of diffusion models is also charged to competition with the other generative methods like GANs and VAEs. As shown with the help of the number of examples based on case studies, It is useful to consider the strengths of diffusion models in terms of the quality of the performed sample and the variability of the coverage; however, it is necessary to compare this method with other options to determine its efficiency and applicability in detail. When it comes to the generative methods, all have their strengths and weaknesses and the choice of which model to use depends on the specific application that is at hand.

It is therefore expected that with the constant development in the area of generative modeling, diffusion models will offer a key contribution towards more complex data generation. Further applications and advancements for diffusion models under discussion include having more constraints to the given tasks or proposing integration of diffusion models with other generative methods. Such developments can be expected to extend the horizons of diffusion models and provide more uses for this model in numerous fields.

These diffusion models are a major improvement to generative modeling, providing a strong paradigm for generating quality and varied data. By generating a sample that undergoes a gradual transition from noise to data, diffusion models are capable of creating quite realistic images with minor differences between each one. Some of the limitations that are present include the computational cost and optimization of noise schedules However, with continuous research and development more advancements are expected to be made that will improve the performance of diffusion models. As a general and efficient generative method, diffusion models will surely leave a great impact on numerous applications including image and audio synthesis, data augmentation, and so on.

7.5 Implementing Generative Models on Embedded Devices

Using generative models for embedded devices is rather motivationally vocal sociotechnical and scientific in the sense that it is one of the most AI-related uses of models, applied directly to instances of tangible experience. Low-powered, small-size devices have been used primarily in roles such as collecting data from sensors and basic controls for several decades. Earlier in time, such functions were too cumbersome for such devices, and were restricted to simpler models; but by using generative modeling methods and by constantly improving the performance of the embedded circuits now such devices can perform complex functions which inter alia include generative models. The integration of these two allows hope in adding new higher layers of machine learning for the edge devices as they advance in latency, efficiency, and privacy.

VAEs, GANs, and the newer diffusion models train a model to figure out a sampling distribution that allows it to generate data that is different from the training data but similar. Some of the utilizes that are seen in various fields include image and audio generation, data enlargement and anomaly detection. They have applied these models to some extent in embedded devices However, the following drawbacks need to be fulfilled while using these models on embedded devices Computational complexity Memory, and Energy constraint.

Thus, the first challenge of generosity is the fact that the cognitive ability to calculate is already present in those embedded devices. They will not be able to compute as compared to the devices used on a desktop or in a server platform. Since the generative models, especially with the help of deep learning algorithms, can be computationally demanding it is crucial to optimize them for the operation in the embedded systems. This can be resolved in various ways such the model quantization which is the process of applying the quantization to the model weights and activations. Quantization also reduces the amount of computation that needs to be performed in a given model as it allows for the use of small data sizes as it occupies better in a device.

Another technique that is used to optimize the computational efficiency of the model is threshold pruning in which the model is pruned of some components which are not as important or are not very crucial to the model. Therefore by either axon or neuron growth cone, excessive interconnections are pruned out and the model is optimized with virtually little impact on the result. This is particularly so where the constraints of using the chip are related to the processing capacities of the device that has the chip installed on it. In addition, from a knowledge transfer point of view, knowledge distillation is that which can be used to transfer the features of a large model to a small efficient one. In this process, there is a training of a lower capacity model to copy the operation of the large model, thus cones with efficiency in power consumption while promoting high-quality solutions.

Another factor that is implicated especially when working with generative models on embedded devices is the question of memory in those kinds of devices. The generative models but more especially the large neural network architectures require memory to store the parameters, the middle computations, and the data. To counter this, efficient architectures of the model such as tensor decomposition are employed during the process. Memory can also be better utilized with the help of what's known as 'rungs' such as FPGAs or ASICs that are optimized for particular AI operations.

Another essential feature as far as generative models are concerned while operating in embedded devices is the power capacity that these devices demand. Some of the connected devices are battery-operated and therefore energy control for purposes of battery conservation ought to embrace the features for sustainable functionality. There is no doubt that simple optimization techniques such as algorithms and computational optimization exercises can significantly help to manage the energy consumption of the model. Another useful strategies that is is dynamic voltage and frequency scaling which operates in the context of power-given workload and energy-aware scheduling.

Regarding the generative models used in the current work on the embedded devices, both aspects of the software and the hardware are incorporated, as well as the integration of both aspects. Some of the real-time operating systems (RTOS) or bare metal, as one may find in embedded systems, may not have the latest machine learning frameworks. Therefore, the way of implementing generative models into these environments may require the usage of a new implementation for the environment itself or even a lighter version of the library. For instance, TensorFlow Lite and ONNX Runtime are the frameworks that deal with the execution of machine learning models on the edges of the network and can be further expanded to include generative models.

Thus, there are two factors, of which the usage of model inference optimization might be regarded as very important. In particular, inference speed is one of the most crucial metrics for applications with strict time requirements as in image or audio generation tasks. Such methods can be used to reduce the time of inference by reducing the amount of mathematical computations to be made as discussed with model quantization earlier. In addition, the use of accelerators for AI such as GPUs,

TPUs, or NPUs will also help to improve the inference rate. Such accelerators are inherently parallel and can boost the throughput of these models by a not insignificant amount.

Some of the general problems that come with training generative models for deployment at the edges of embedded devices are data privacy/Security. Thus, the embedded devices are frequently located in the environment where the confidential data are collected and processed. To this end, it becomes important to ensure that generative models are not a threat to the users' data. The three methods which include on-device encryption, boot encryption, and trusted execution environment (TEE) have the potential of supporting the protection of data integrity and confidentiality. Besides, the local training model and updating techniques which are also secure for the subjects' data include federated learning.

However, there are certain significant benefits of applying the generative models on embedded devices. This in turn increases efficiency as data processing is done locally and not transferred to other servers hence reducing latency. This is highly optimal, especially in the context of real-time and near real-time applications, for example: augmented reality, autopilot vehicles, and video games. This way, embedded devices can limit the amount of information that is transferred over the network and can generate data on their own which makes them capable of providing superior and more timely user experience.

The other advantage is that using data in the process does not have to go to other servers for analysis and processing. This is especially true with applications where the data collected is of high sensitivity, or where the identity of the user has to be highly protected such as in health monitoring, or as a security measure. This gets rid of the scenario whereby the service provider has complete control over your data by storing it within the device hence reducing susceptibility to data loss.

Last but not least, it is possible to apply generative models in embedded devices and it is likely to lead to the optimization of the whole system and decrease the frequency of utilization of network bandwidth. Local generation and processing of data at the devices themselves mean less communication of data over the network and hence; lesser costs for the communication and also less congestion of the network. This goes well, especially in places where network connection is a little bit scarce or costly.

The application of generative models on embedded devices is a remarkable improvement in the domain of edge computing and AI. By exploring computational problems, memory issues, and energy consumption on instruments and by utilizing the approach of quantization, weight pruning, and knowledge distillation, it is possible to integrate complicated generative models in devices with fewer resources. That is why this approach is very attractive to reduce the latency time, to increase the privacy level, and to optimize the system performance for numerous applications. Because advancement in technology is inevitable, the inclusion of generative models in embedded systems is expected to grow common and hence provide more viable solutions that can be implemented in different fields.

7.6 Applications and Use Cases

Although generative models were initially path models, they have found various other uses in many disciplines; They have disruptive potential to generate similar new data similar to real-life examples. These models do not only make alterations in the design of the data generation process but also provide several applications in several fields. Whether in creative aspects of media and entertainment to even enhancement of scientific and industrial advancements, one can see such generative models as potentially serving as a valuable assortment indeed.

However, in the context of creativity and applying generative models in the media and entertainment industry, a has been significant progress. For instance, to generate new images in visual arts and designs, GANs and VAEs models have been used for inventing other forms of art that do not belong to the real world as real-world scientists and designers use them to invent new images, designs, and patterns which are not real in the real world. For example, GANs have been used to generate fake images of people's faces, scenes, landscapes, and even whole scenes that look as if it was real photos. This capability could be applied in video game designing among other fields where designing impressive and eye-popping graphics is relevant.

Similarly, in the field of music and audio synthesis, generative models have been applied to create new songs or to copy a particular style of music or other sounds. This is because one can train models that generate tunes, chords, and beats with samples from a certain genre or style from a large database. This has led to the formation of new creations of new soundtracks and the instruments of musicians and composers to develop new novel concepts and to present new auditory concepts. For example, new compositions created by AI can be used in film music, advertisement, and games providing new and fresh sound opportunities.

The generative models in natural language processing are doing the cadena between the old and the new – the new way of engaging with texts and language. Certain language models which include The generative pre-trained transformer (GPT) have done to one that is capable of delivering contextually a presented text. These models are applied in various fields such as when developing bots, writing pieces, or personalizing the messages. For example, it can be used in generative models for creating outlines for articles, for the development of conversational interface bots, which mimic real-life interpersonal interactions, or even for developing models of how to answer clients' complaints department. This has the potential not only to make the creation of content efficient but also the interaction through these more intriguing as well as flexible.

Generative models are heavily involved in this aspect in the sense that they offer direct synthetic healthcare data that can be useful to researchers and developers. Because of privacy regulations, it can be challenging to employ these real data in other learning models; thus, synthetic data that are generated with the help of these models can be used for training machine learning, simulations, or for developing the proper diagnostic instruments. For instance, generative models can vytvořit umělá Sheila's medical images which possess the same statistical properties as the images of patients But these are fake images hence Sheila's identity is not compromised. From it, synthetic data can be used in the validation and training of algorithms for diagnosing diseases design of treatment regimes, and the development of individual treatment programs for a particular patient.

It is also worth noting that generative models also have its applications in the drug development process in phylactery. Quite literally, drug discovery refers to the search for a molecule that is yet to be discovered but has the potential of contributing positively to the field of health care delivery. As such, generative models particularly the deep learning generative model can be used in the generation of new chemical entities and perhaps provide a glimpse of how the compounds under consideration will behave with biochemical targets. Such an approach accelerates the process of searching the new drugs since it is possible to test numerous variants at the same time and accept or reject them significantly quicker which is valuable for the treatment of diseases.

These types of generative models are today being used in the field of processes as well as industrial manufacturing in terms of designs together with workflow. For instance, in additive manufacturing well known as 3D printing format, generative design algorithms can develop innovative and optimum format which is hard to be detected under conventional design methodologies. These models are capable of generating design solutions that can be customized to meet certain needs with minimal usage of material and at the same time offer optimum performance. This capability is useful in aerospace, automotive, and consumer goods industries mainly because elegant as well as optimal solutions are mostly the aim.

The generative models are also starting to appear in the sphere of finance and economics at the same speed. These domains use models when creating the simulation of financial markets, predicting evolutions of them and even generating realistic synthetic financial values. Based on historical and statistical data, modes generative can build several potential schemes of the market conditions which, in turn, can be useful in the assessment of the risk and potential of the portfolio as well as in the development of necessary strategies. Besides, these models will have synthetic data for experimenting and testing the financial algorithms in a way that enhances the stability of the financial systems.

Other related fields that the generative models have focused on include data consolidation and anomaly detection. In data augmentation, generative models allow for generating new training samples from the set of data thereby improving the performance and generalization ability of machine learning. This is especially the case when collecting a vast amount of sample data to label them is challenging and/or expensive. For instance, generative models can generate new images/text thus enhancing the form of the training data.

The other approach that can be used in anomaly detection is the generative approach where the overall behavior is learned and then any divergent behavior is identified. These have implications in cases like fraud denying, network securing, and predicting the time to maintenance. Therefore, the generative models can identify the characteristics that signify abnormal data and it is possible to consider such data points as future issues or threats.

However, it is envisaged that the fair usage of generative models could open a can of numerous applications and use cases, thus, certain ethical as well as practical questions need to be answered. For instance, because it is possible to create virtually human talking heads, issues arise over the genuineness of information found on the internet. Transparency and correct application can play quite an important role so that generative models would not be misused or used for the publishing of false information. Further, generating models are also used in sensitive areas like health care and finance have implications for data privacy, security, and rules and regulations.

Altogether, generative models are proliferating and revolutionizing different sectors in terms of content generation and data processing as well as prediction. Due to their capability to produce large quantities of accurate and varied data, the technologies are revolutionary and offer a prospect for enhancement in various fields. Due to technological advancement and the now-growing presence of generative models across diverse fields, the possibilities for improvising the current use of generative models, as well as the effects and hardships that come with them, are seemingly unending.

CHAPTER 8: CASE STUDIES IN EMBEDDED DEEP LEARNING

8.1 Healthcare and Medical Devices

In the medical practice the use of advanced technology is prevalent in both health care delivery systems and health care equipment. These changes are brought about by artificial intelligence, machine learning and embedded systems that advance the diagnostic capabilities, improve on treatment and provide more customers' specific solutions to the medical facilities. Among all these fields of development, there is perhaps the least amount of doubt about the practical application of advanced models and technologies as medical devices.

An area that has been revolutionized with incredible potential by the use of artificial intelligence in the conduct of its operations is that of diagnosis imaging. Magnetic resonance imaging, computed tomography, and radiography are among the important diagnostic modalities that are noninvasive in the diagnosis of most diseases in medicine. There are various deep learning algorithms constructed to analyze medical images with rather high accuracy. These sorts of algorithms can be used in order to make conclusions that can point at the existence of certain diseases including cancer, various neurological disorders, and numerous cardiovascular ailments. For instance, instead of doing diagnosis on x-rays or MRI scans, the AI driven software will mark or point out areas that needs to be examined more by the radiologists. It also helps in diagnosis as well as identification of the abnormalities that are very crucial to management of diseases.

Apart from image analysis within diagnostics, AI is already influencing predictive analysis and risk assessment. Using data from electronic health records (EHRs), it is possible to develop large sets of models that would determine trends and make prognosis. These models can predict the diseases in probability terms, monitor its advance stage, and identify potential treatment manageable corresponding to patients' information. For example, prediction may be used in the probability of getting the chronic diseases including diabetes or cardiac diseases and this leaves plenty of precaution. These factors also help in additional control of the ailment and save a lot of costs and burden on the health care facilities.

Everyone agrees that AI-enabled and embedded medical devices along with telemedicine and remote monitoring are also changing the medical world. Smartwatches and fitness trackers are calculated to track biosignals, including heart rate, blood pressure, and oxygen saturation levels for constant stream. These devices are used for monitoring in real time health conditions that need physical intervention, data that can be feed into artificial intelligence for diagnosis. For instance, whereas using ECG wrist-worn devices can detect even the slightest pattern of any perturbation in normal heart rhythm that may be characteristic of some types of cardiac conditions. This capability enhances the facility of remote patient adherence, a factor that is useful in conditions that need constant observation of the patients. It is crucial in delivering the continuation of care and ongoing management with the patients that enable the health care departments to reduce direct contact and scale the efforts at delivering care.

AI & machine-learning is also in forefront of innovation in personalized medicine especially in genomics & precision medicines. AI models are applied to decode people's genes and determine the genetic markers of specific disease or disorders. Its use would involve developing differential therapeutic management strategies with different patients depending on their genetic makeup. For instance, the AI algorithms can be used to analyze the genomic data to determine how a given patient will be likely to fare when given a given medication so as to reduce the side effects of the medication while at the same time increasing their efficiency. This improves the overall medical results of treatments and consequently reduces negative side effects per patient.

Diagnostic instruments are also seeing gains coming from improved AI's decision assistance technology. These systems help the healthcare providers arrive at the right decision because the recommendation provided is based on research findings. For instance, decision support systems can help evaluate patient information, his or her history, and current research to arrive at the best treatment approach of the patient or recommended tests. This support is rather helpful in those cases that require analyzing many factors simultaneously. The advantages of the use of these systems are that these helps support the overall HI, the health care information, the health care professional and the patient these aspects to reduce the risks of a decision making as well as augment the quality of care.

But there is also a need for information that linked with the utilization of smart medical devices, data privateness and security. The data that is collected in the medical field is so sensitive and as a result it must be protected in the best way possible. AI models utilized in medical devices are required by law to meet specific policy rules of data protection to avoid the exposure of patient data. A number of rights that limit information access as well as protection and management of information and files as its custodians can contribute a lot to information security. Also, the transparency and explainability of AI models is important to gain trust with the directly involved healthcare providers and to make sure that one understands the basis for a decision.

The other concern is the permanency of convincing and constantly checking AI-based models in the used medical devices. AI algorithms may not be as efficient because, apart from changes in distribution of relevant information, there have been updates in the medical science. That is why the ongoing validation and updating are needed to ensure the validity and stability of the AI use in medical applications. However, this necessitates constant testing of these models, repopulating models with new data and the feedback of the healthcare providers.

Nevertheless, there are also many possibilities of using AI as well as the other advanced technologies for the enhancement of the healthcare situation. Bathing big data, discovering patterns, and creating tools and strategies for arriving at improved insights shows potential to revolutionize patient treatment plans and enhance health outcomes. The use of real-life diagnosis and treatment and possibly even through integration of artificial intelligence and embedded systems promises to enhance diagnostics, reliably personalize treatment and even enhance the delivery of care through reliable medical devices.

In the next years, the future of healthcare and medical devices will largely depend on the further evolution of AI, machine learning and embed factors. AI will bring new ideas as robotic surgery, smart implants, and improved telehealth solutions, and grasp new opportunities for patient care and benefit. These technologies, if incorporated in the medical devices, will demand the effort of authors, developers, and health care providers to facilitate the development and implementation of the technologies.

AI and embedded systems are a groundbreaking step in the system of healthcare and medical devices. From improving the diagnosis through imaging and predicting patient outcomes to remote and personalized medicine technologies are bringing major changes in the field of medicine. That is why, the issues, linked with data privacy or security, and model validation, are crucial to resolve to achieve successful application of AI in the Medical Devices' field. Technology is set to go up and so the chances of enhancing healthcare delivery and patient's results through innovative medical devices will also go up thus offering a potent for further improving the results of patient care and the field.

8.2 Autonomous Vehicles and Drones

The idea of self-driving cars and drones is the new innovation that has occurred for the manufacture of transport and robotics. These technologies based on artificial intelligence, machine learning, and embedded systems are revolutionizing the way we build, control, and communicate with technological surroundings, offering new chances to increase general over efficiency, security, and convenience. Since the abilities of autonomous systems are steadily progressing, people have to face new captivating opportunities for Apply in different fields of life.

An example of such a social-scientific advancement in technology, is the occurrence of Self-Driving cars, also known as: autonomous vehicles. Many of these automobiles employ such things as sensors, cameras, radar frequencies, and even complicated algorithms to steer and select other aspects of the vehicle operation by themselves. Autonomous vehicles are a system where computer vision on the object is used for its identification, deep learning for reaching decision and the superior control system is used for the control of objects. Self-driven vehicles use information obtained from their environment to determine the presence of objects and signals on the road and changes in traffic flow.

The use of the automobiles with the help of artificial intelligence is very promising. From the security point of view, they provide the potential for reducing traffic accidents due to such factors as drunk driving or distraction. The use of powerful sensors and AI algorithm to observe the vehicle's environment and make correct control decisions will improve road safety in general. Besides, these vehicles can enhance traffic management as well as minimize congestion by incorporating the best approaches toward the route association with other vehicles.

Apart from safety, seven principles of convenience and accessibility can be enhanced through the usage of autonomous vehicles. For people with disabilities and, more generally, for those who cannot drive, self-driving cars have the potential to unleash a new kind of mobility. Furthermore, we also have an opportunity of making transport more efficient by having features like self- driving cars for hire and self-driving delivery trucks. Concerning the identified change, its achievement carries the potential for the revision of urban movement and ultimately the scaled decrease in reliance on cars.

Unmanned Aerial Vehicles (UAVs) or drones are another innovation that has numerous use; it refers to an aircraft operated without any onboard crew. Unmanned aerial vehicles also possess a number of sensors and cameras which enable it to take aerial photographs, observe conditions and execute activities with differed accuracy. Some of facts which make them useful are; Being able to work under different conditions makes them useful in various fields of economies.

Precision farming can also be identified as one of the major application area of drones for agriculture where crop health, the condition of the soil and the usage of resource are given high attention. By taking photographs of a relatively high resolution and data analysis, drones can assist the farmers in choosing an optimal time to water the crops, apply fertilizers or fight pests. They are also important in raising yields, minimizing wastage and in encouraging environmentally-friendly farming, and for this reason they are being embraced by farmers.

In areas of inspection particularly infrastructure, drones prove to be an efficient and cost-friendly way of serving such structures like bridges, power lines and pipelines. In the past, these inspections entailed considerable man power and were often associated with certain levels of safety hazard. Robots integrated with higher quality cameras and sensors can provide aerial views of the sites in need of inspection and this can greatly help in providing solutions to likely problems as well as minimizing the need for physically visiting the areas. This capability does not only enhance safety but also offer flexibility in conduct more frequent a nd rigorous assessment on infrastructure assets.

emergency response and disaster management is another area where utilization of drones is seen, further applications. The drones are used to give the streaming footage of the disaster-affected regions for its operation in search and rescue and assessment of the impact. For instance, during disaster conditions such as hurricanes or earthquakes then drone can quickly survey areas that have been destroyed by disaster thereby helping in, rescues services and help in making distributions of aid items. Their work of extending for such areas just to ensure they are delivering supplies, or in basic need, which is medical attention which can greatly contribute the difference between life and death is very important and could help in the healing process.

Similarly the large UAVs have also been perceived desirable especially in logistics and Shuttle Services. There is emerging discussion on the last-mile delivery whereby firms use drones to deliver customer consignments directly to their homes. It has implications for delivery time reduction, cost cutting and traffic congestion in the congested urban environment. Through making delivery process faster, drones can also help reduce the time to navigate the supply chain by fixing the most optimal routes.

Nevertheless, there are some challenges and conditions that must be considered in the case of tolerable uses of autonomous cars and drones. With reference to the problematics of the autonomous vehicles, safety countertypes and reliability countertypes play the most critical role. This is done to assess the responsiveness of the self-driving system to different real-life conditions and to check whether the right action will be taken should any of the events happen. Further, it is essential to create the corresponding legal requirements and codes – choice of risk, liability and insurance, and data protection.

For drones, control of the airspace and guarantee of the secure and proper operation of the aircraft in the airspace is always an issue. Growing use of drones creates the need for the formulation of principles to help avoid accidents, intrusion of privacy, and security threats. Connection to legacy air traffic control systems and creating technologies to avoid midair collisions and to manage traffic are also crucial elements of improving the safety of drones.

self-driving cars and unmanned aerial vehicles are two that cause moral and sociotechnical concerns about when and how they are used. Several chain questions arise with large implications like job displacement, privatization of data, and displacement of traditional industries. As these technologies advance, there should be dialogues that encompass their impact and positivity found ways to solve problems so that the gains that comes with these technologies are tapped in to the full.

Automated cars and drones are new innovative technologies, which are relatively young but already have the aim to revolve around many sectors and industries. These inventions cover a lot of areas from improving road safety and efficiency of transportation to changing the whole course of agriculture and supply chain. However, handling the problems of safety, regulatory, and ethical questions makes it quite real to transform such people to become useful citizens in the society. In the future, when new technologies appear in transportation and other industries, self-driving cars and drones will have a greater and more powerful potential.

8.3 Industrial IoT

The Industrial Internet of Thing is a remarkable shift where industries are fully transformed by the growing technological aspects within them including sensors, connectivity and data analytics. It is bringing significant changes into industry through increasing intelligence, efficiency and connectivity of processes in countless fields. Fundamentally, I-IoT harnesses the capabilities of constantly interconnected devices and systems to acquire data and processes it concurrently, which results in optimization of processes and organizations, intelligent maintenance, and novel business models.

Instrumental in I-IoT is the use of sensors and actuators on the industrial systems and devices. These devices capture significant information about the physical environment and its conditions such as temperature, pressure, vibration and geographical position. This data is then transferred to other central processor to make analysis on what has been collected. I-IoT systems are always monitoring equipment performance to give insights into the conditions or other performance indicators. This real-time visibility helps business to identify anomalies, address problem areas and even improve processes and workflows in ways that would not have been possible earlier.

Among all the advantages of the I-IoT, the application in the area of prediction of the maintenance requirement is the most important one. Many businesses continue to follow the conventional method of turning equipment maintenance into a routine by conducting periodic inspections or repairing whenever equipment fails. I-IoT alters this way of working by applying intelligent analysis in an attempt to estimate when an item is likely to develop a fault or need repair. Real-time performance analysis in addition to historical performance can reveal patterns that may show that some part of the process is about to fail or go wrong. This approach brings about timely interferences, cuts on the probabilities of having unplanned avoidance of time and increases the usage time of equipment's. For instance, in manufacturing, the I-IoT sensors can track the overall health of equipment and help provide signals to operators and technicians when they should prepare to change out or repair a piece of equipment to avoid a system shutdown or breakdown.

Another interesting area of I-IoT is its use in improving business's operational performance. In this way, I-IoT allows businesses to gather live information about their efforts, investigate process problems, solve them, and enhance efficiency of utilization of resources. For instance, while using I-IoT on the energy segment, it is possible to track how energy generation units and the energy distribution network work so that appropriate control can be made to enhance energy utilization. In the same way, I-IoT in supply chain management can sort stocks, check the state of the goods in freight, and adjust the delivery trajectory. Notwithstanding this high level of control and visibility, the companies are aided to make right decisions, avert wastage, and enhance organizational productivity.

Integration of I-IoT also helps in creating big data and analytics for machine learning model. This makes a lot of sense because ample data means that businesses can feed complex algorithms to get patterns, outcomes and solutions. For instance, machine learning can use past records of production to make a prediction on the demand, scheduling and enhancing quality. Besides, there may be some tendencies that can escape the analyst' attention, and AI in that case can provide a better understanding of the operations and more ways to improve them.

I-IoT is also helping to create new forms of businesses and services. Through obtaining and processing data in real time, I-IoT enables creating new business models and high added value services, such as remote monitoring, diagnostics, performance-based contracts, data-based consultancy services. For example, in industries that use production equipment, equipment makers can provide ongoing maintenance to those customers through I-IoT hence ensuring that their products work optimally throughout their useful life. This change from more conventional ownership models towards service-oriented models is a fundamental change of operations of companies towards their clients.

However, several challenges and factors arising from the implementation of I-IoT are worth discussing below. Of all these concerns, there is only one that merits major discussion and that is the question of data security. With the I-IoT explaining higher connected and data trading, there are additional risk factors and threats. Preserving that which must remain confidential and guaranteeing that industrial platforms cannot be compromised by cyberelements is important. There is a wide agreement that the implementation of encryption, access control, and realization of security audit policies to work is crucial to protect I-IoT systems, and, respectively, customers' confidence.

One of the key issues is integration of I-IoT with current industrial systems and applications. Most companies still work with systems inherited from other periods, often with no allowance for connections or data sharing. Converting these systems as to include and integrate I-IoT technologies can be a rather expensive and challenging process. It is crucial for companies to properly manage the compatibility issues with the intention of creating a sound implementation plan for I-IoT that will not disrupt the functionality of its business.

However, it is only possible to deploy I-IoT when qualified human resources are available for data analysis, cyber protection and industry automation. This is why it becomes crucial that competent people be hired to analyze and interpret data generated by the new I-IoT technologies. There is always a need to train and develop people within organizations in order to get the right skills and competencies with organizations.

In future the development of I-IoT is expected to be driven by the evolution of other technologies like edge computing and 5G communication. Configuration of more data at the edge (I-IoT) may improve the performance of the I-IoT system by temporarily minimizing latency magnitudes. In the same manner, 5G is a technology that bestows higher and more stable connection to the I-IoT applications and expands the ranges of their operations.

In conclusion, the Industrial Internet of Things is a new concept of change that defines a new way of fashioning industries and their business surrounding them. The value of I-IoT is realized by improving connected devices, doing real-time analysis of data that these devices generate, together with improving the equipment and business processes. Despite the ones aforementioned concerning security, integration as well as the personnel, I-IoT is capable of producing the following benefits. As the technology advances, I-IoT will remain a pivot as far as the future of industrial operations and the advancement of advancing technology is concerned.

8.4 Smart Home Devices

Smart home devices are changing the world and our lives for the better, making our lives more convenient and safer, and helping us save money on our utilities. Some of these devices put into practice artificial intelligence, IoT, and embedded systems to command and automate more complex life processes. Slowly but steadily manufacturers and developers of smart home technology are changing the way we live in our homes, they bring convenience and enjoyable experiences into homes.

In essence, there are devices at the center of smart home technology through which the homeowner can manage the different parts of their homes from a distance. Such everyday devices as smart thermostats are several steps ahead of traditional heating- and cooling-only systems. They incorporate features of machine learning to update temperatures in accordance with user habits and preferences for making the living environment comfortable, as well as conserving energy. Smart thermostats can be initialized through apps or voice commands which means that users can get back home to a well-conditioned house even without adjusting the settings physically.

Another of the technological advances seen in home automation relates to the use of smart lighting systems. They can be managed by the use of apps, voice control, or programmed timetables from smart phones or even through voice commands. Smart bulbs can also be dimmed and have tunable white light, it's possible to achieve any desired lighting scene. In addition, smart lighting also addresses the security factor where the house can be made to look occupied each time homeowners are out of the house. They also do the same with the lighting where they are able to have them controlled by motion sensors so that they switch on and /or off depending on the motion detected and this one is preferred since it saves power.

Smart devices make most improvements within home security, which is a very important area. Other components of smart security are security cameras, motion sensors, and video doorbells that allow homeowners monitor their homes in real-time. Most of these devices are intelligent and hence can be operated from a distance; that way, it is easier to monitor the property at any one time and promptly act on any violation of security. Also, smart locks do not require keys and have the setting of remote access, which is a major benefit since both aspects –

security and convenience are improved. All these devices make those essential contributions to other smart home systems to create a security network that offers people reassurance.

Integration with the smart home gadgets which ranges from voice recognition gadgets such as Google Home and Amazon Alexa, also work in the favor of the product. It specifies that users can use specific words to control their smart devices with voice instructions to ease the operation of multiple features in a home. While telling an appropriate lighting level and temperature, or playing a specific song or setting a reminder, they also allow for easy interaction and use of smart home systems. This approach simplifies the using process and makes technologies for home automation more available to anyone.

Another very importance feature is energy management in smart home. Smart plugs and energy monitors allow the homeowners to see overtime which device consumes much power thus help in energy saving. The users can track when exactly the devices are most active and if they use more energy to set the schedule and turn them on/off appropriately. For example, smart plugs used in appliances can be set to switch off when the appliances are not required while energy monitors may also provide log books for energy consumption in the house. Besides, reducing costs, it also promotes environmental conservation since resource utilization is optimized.

Smart home devices also, make contribution in providing comfort and ease to the daily life. For instance, controlling of window blinds can operate automatically to control the time of day or the intensity of a light in a room and they are efficient on energy conservation as well as user comfort. Fridges, cookers, washing machines offer characteristics such as mobility and the capability to control chores done at home from a distance. For instance, it is possible to set the smart oven for preheating from a remote location or to set a washing machine in the process of a particular cycle of washing so that the users do not have to bear the burden of household chores and thus; endure more these everyday tasks.

The symbiosis of smart home systems with health and wellbeing is a relatively new area, which opens a great potential for development. Smart air purifiers and water quality sensors are approved ways that we ensure the indoor environment we live in is clean to enhance our quality living. Combined with smart home technologies, wearable health devices can monitor people's vital signs and activity levels, the information of which can help inform people's wellbeing. All of these advancements tend to add feature and richness to the aspects of self-care and home health management.

When many have embraced the idea of smart home devices there are some factors which needs to be taken. This is an important factor whereby different devices in use will need to interplay with the other in an efficient manner. Since there are many manufacturers and several technologies being implemented, it becomes important that smart products from different manufacturers are compatible for unity on the smart home. This interoperability can only be attained when there are standardized protocol and platform in place giving the users a standard and reliable system.

Other point which user have to consider are the privacy and security issue of smart home technology as well. The application of personal data and their transfer through smart devices seem neither less significant to the subject of data protection and potential concerns. Evaluating and implementing effective security features in the devices include encrypting the devices, as well as implementing secure authentication devises is paramount when it comes to protection of users' information. Also, users should be aware of data collection practices with regard to their information and be able to decide how that information can be used and disseminated.

Nevertheless, the advantages of smart home devices are huge and increase each day because of the improvement in the technology. The lumens that smart home technologies are capable to improve such parameters as convenience, security, energy, and quality of life makes this decision appealing to many homeowners. In those cases, the smart home ecosystem will keep on growing and as new and new innovations appear the home ecosystem will provide even more useful features that are compatible with people's lives.

smart home systems are changing the face of human life by offering innovative elements of control and energy saving. Therefore, these technologies help to enhance the level of comfort and security of the residents, to energy efficiency and health issues which reveal the sphere of an enriching human life. As the smart home industry expands, engineering approaches to key issues will be critical in creating positive consumer experiences for Smart Home. The emergence of smart home technology also depicts the future trends and adaptation as a result improving the quality of life within homeowners.

8.5 Wearable Technology

Wearable technology has rapidly turned into a strategic innovation in individual wellbeing and lifestyle. Products such as smartwatches, fitness trackers, and even advanced smart clothing present the opportunity to facilitate the control and optimization of day-to-day functioning in a manner like has never been possible before. From being seen as tools for the select few to being deemed as necessities of life, wearables owe their shift to the size, sensitivity, and smarts of electronics.

The foundation of wearable technology lies in the actual monitoring of a number of health indicators in real time. Smart watches and some of the fitness trackers for instance, their sensors are capable of tracking both physical activities including, steps, distance covered, and caloric output. They also collect entire physiological information of a person such as rate of pulse, sleep cycle, even blood oxygen level. Due to the capability of acquiring this data consecutively, wearables present users with essential information with reference to health and fitness, in setting and accomplishing people'sational milestones. For example, walking a fixed number of steps on a daily basis can encourage a person to take more steps and thus obtaining a healthy lifestyle; or monitoring the hours of sleep daily can help a person, get better sleep by recognizing the sleeping pattern.

The incorporation of wearable technology with health monitoring isn't limited to mere health and fitness tracking. Current wearables also encompass additional features in healthcare surveillance that existing wearables do not have such as a continuous glucose monitoring for diabetic patients and ECG to monitor improper heart rhythms. These features help users to better control their diseases, as well as make correct decision on their treatment. For instance, there is a smart bracelet that is designed to have ECG sensors and keep track of the user and notify that he or she has atrial fibrillation that needs medical intervention. That kind of health monitoring may help a person identify slight risks of developing an illness and get medical help before experiencing complications.

In consumer electronics there are also many effects in all aspects of safety and security increased. Technological products include smartwatches with GPS and emergency call help security since they support and protect the life of the user in case of any calamity. For instance, several smartwatches come with fall detection sensors that may immediately notify the emergency contacts, or services, in the event that the user has a fall. An example is when it is features such as this – older population or people with certain medical conditions that may lead to falls. Non-contact communication with the possibility of orientation with the position of the person and the possibility of calling an emergency increases the level of individual security and confidence.

Apart from health risk and safety, we have seen that the concept of wearable technology has greatly advanced with regards to the comfort of the person wearing a device and communications. Smartwatches and fitness bands have built in compatibility with smartphone, whereby users can reply to messages, change songs, and draw app control directly from their wrists. This connection cuts down the times one has to be glued to a phone, they make the communication process easy thus improving the experience of users. Interfaced wearables also increase accessibility because they work almost hands-free and can be run through basic voice directions. It illustrates this level of integration as a way to enhance wearable technology in the sense of moving beyond niche and complicated into easier to use and therefore more impactful in our day-to-day lives.

The category of wearable electronics is also extending to smart clothing as well. These apparels incorporate electrodes and are designed from textile that can sense several varieties of human physiologic variables such as heart rate, temperature, and muscle contractions. These garments include information display during certain activities such as exercising; this can help the athletes achieve their best and avoids cases of injuries. For example, a wearable smart-shirt for runner may include monitoring of muscle stiffness and posture that may provide useful running tips and prevent overuse injuries. The concepts behind smart clothing show promise in extending their elements to the realms of enhanced fitness and, especially, medicine as an organic extension of everyday wear.

As with any new technology, there are many benefits but also potential problems Where the use of wearable technology is concerned. One of the key issues is privacy and security of information and particulars of patients and or customers. Smart devices track health and personal information and need an efficient security measure to secure the data. Measures which can be applied here include encryption of the data, proper authentication, and subsequent improvements made in the updates of the software to provide safe protection to the users' data and to regain the faith of the people. there always needs to be guidelines on how the data will be used and, on its collection, too, if the data is being collected from a user, then the user's permission has to be sought.

An issue that may be thought of is whether such gadgets present precision on their outcomes. What is noteworthy is that many current devices have additional features to help track data, but the measurement accuracy in such cases does not always meet expectations and can depend on the device location and the user's activity. Intuitiveness, Interpretability, Quality of data are key factors that make wearables effective and IT resources essential for wearables to deliver accurate and consistent results. Manufacturers therefore have the responsibility of testing and validating their devices in order to be certain that they are accurate and efficient.

Wearable technology has great potential and future development remains to be unveiled. Future trends related to wearables include the production of better health sensors, further integration with other smart devices, growth in software related to new areas such as augmented and virtual reality and real immersion. Smartwatches may be able to progress to even more seamlessly fit into the average consumer's life and provide even more features that can help improve people's lives across the board.

Wearable technology is making significant impact in personal health, safety as well as convenience going into the future. Self-monitoring of health and fitness tracking, disease and illness management, improved connectivity, and seamless integration into smart clothes are these devices various advantages that improve individuals' lives. Expectations such as privacy, accuracy, and data integration issue will be critical in the determination of the success of wearable technology. In future innovations, wearable devices will only be established to be more of a necessity that will create more possibilities in

adding values to people's health, safety as well as
their well-being.

8.6 Success Stories and Lessons Learned

Numerous examples of technology and innovation successes can be useful in achieving higher results and learning from available resources in overcoming challenges. These stories not only increase awareness of achievements of nominees and occasional visitors to the Web site but also explain what has been gained through their experience. This allows viewing of different success stories, the analysis of which will show threads and patterns favorable for success while also considering the difficulties encountered on the way to success.

Another example is the company that initiated the shift to a new generation of consumer electronics introducing a smartphone. When the first smartphone was released, they were a landmark improvement from the common cell phones of that time with a variety of features other than voice. The impetus of this innovation was from a dream to build a single device, or a product that had aspects of mobile computing, internet connectivity among other add-ons right from multi-media, in one product that users could interact with easily. This smartphone was a big success not necessarily because of the technology it was built with but because of how it incorporated user friendly interface, simplicity, and compatibility with other software services. The factors that can be suggested resulting from this success include, focused strategies toward acknowledging the customer's needs, use of single unified products that can perform many roles and draw from experience, the impact of continuously developing new features.

A more exciting story is when a firm developed an artificial intelligence (AI) based company and became an industry giant through it. It created a platform that is based on artificial intelligence, and its principle was to optimize the companies' operations and their decision-making. Through the big and detailed dataset fed through machine learning algorithms, the platform delivered tangible statistics that boosted efficiency of business activity and strengthened their position in the market. In a nutshell, the success of this AI-driven solution provided some critical lessons which are; There is no substitute to quality of data required, the algorithms must be sound and powerful, and last but not the least, the pace of technological advancements should be well matched and in sync with the business requirements. Moreover, it islands how an important tool be used to solve a main problem and generate value within a broad range of industries.

As the wellbeing of patients is an important part of healthcare to oversee the development and implementation of technologies such as wearable devices have been essential. The latter in this case is illustrated by the story of a firm that developed a bracelet that can capture monitors the physiological indices of a patient and supply live health information to the patient and his or her physicians. This technology made it easier to diagnose, work on, manage and treat these diseases and show better results compared to previous years. I believe wearable technology has proven the effectiveness of having a health monitoring system in relation to a user-friendly interface, the necessity for continuous testing and validation, and the role of wearable devices in closing gaps in healthcare systems.

The uptake of electric vehicles (EV's) is another major example of innovation that has taken root in the industry transformation. The relatively recent innovation of high-performance, long-range EVs has revolutionized the automotive segment by addressing sustainability, as well as consumers' needs and wants. This was due to progress made in the battery systems, the electric drive trains and sustainability values that were upheld. Key factors such as the research and development of new technologies, setting up of charging points for electric vehicles and synchronization of business plans with social objectives are all lessons learnt from the growth of electric vehicles.

Software development is one of the fields where open-source project proves that the collaboration of the public is the key for success. This project involved developing a common software interface that is accepted by use developers across the world. Due to the creative commons approach adopted in the project, the project was able to benefit from the various skills of the community and not only gain fast growth and adoption. This blows up of the open-source project serves to illustrate the importance of the community incentive approach, openness and the social impact of technology.

Some of these stories are merged of numerous success factors and while their objectives are different, here are some of the common success factors that are evident. Product and solution requirements are best determined when there is a clear understanding of the user needs of a certain market. Only through constant generation of new courses of action and the changes, adjustments, and adaptations needed to deal with potential threats and capture new opportunities can firms defeat competition and find a way through the obstacles of new markets. Also, true integration with the actual business application and operations can, in fact, make a difference and generate real value.

But it is clear that no success is accomplished without some problems and these stories also provide information on the real problems. For example, issues such as privacy and security relating to the management of information of such nature are focal point matters as technology that captures such data is developed. Meeting these criteria to the latter can make users have confidence in the quality of products and solutions they proffer which makes them relevant. Moreover, the implementation of technology in the fashion that has potentials of solving some business and societal uses and goals would secure long-term sustainability and benefits for the society.

This paper focuses on success stories in technology and innovation to determine what is being done right and what was learnt in the process. These stories will also help us to identify such values as vision, innovation and user orientation as the key to success within the context of a dynamic and unpredictable environment. Just as we have these success stories, they also address the problems that were encountered and how they could be solved in the event of future events. In future as technology becomes even more sophisticated and new opportunities come allying from space, these success stories will serve as reference in future innovations.

CHAPTER 9: ETHICAL
CONSIDERATIONS AND CHALLENGES

9.1 Bias and Fairness in AI

The two concepts of bias and fairness in the development of Artificial intelligence (AI) is an important issue which has been widely discussed as of the application of AI in many fields of the society. AI negation: Help industries for the better, assists in making decisions, and makes people's lives better; Causes: Produces new bias and enforces existing bias if not controlled. This is very important because it wants to solve some of the main issues that are hampering the right implementation and usage of the AI technologies in a fair way.

The two basic premis which form the center of discussion related to bias into AI and ML are – first, AI systems are trained on data and second, this data contains historical and social bias. That might be due to historical issues of representation, demographic issues, or even some random decision made during data aggregation or data preprocessing stages. For example, if an AI model has been trained under a sample that is biased in some way towards certain groups/individuals then it is probable that the system will make bias decisions/bias. It also leads to injustice because dominance means discrimination in a society in cases of employment, credit, or prosecution.

Bias in AI technology is rife and one of the most widely known is the utilization of algorithms in the hiring of employees. AI system pre-disposed to being trained on biased datasets and particularly certain data from a company record that for example has a record of discrimination on gender or race it will preserve the bias. This leads to diversity and a lack of the representative employment opportunities, as the system just repeats the bias. Likewise, facial recognition systems have been found to give higher errors for people with darker skin tone thereby, calling for balanced training data sets.

The exploit of bias in AI is also pointed out, in the previous section, as having multiple layers that requires addressing. One such strategy is to make sure the data being fed to AI is as diverse as the society in respect to the intended utilization." This involves searching for data from a large number of sources and then critically analyzing it for any issue of sample bias and sample distribution bias respectively. Moreover, the basic measures designed to prevent bias during the model training phase has to be applied. For example, one may train models with convective constraints such that known prejudices within the datasets are corrected or control the type of results containing prejudices during model development.

Another aspect that is important as equity is openness of artificial intelligence and operations.

Owners of AI and related development and organizations should share how they are creating the AI, including data input and rules set, in order to be audited and cross-checked by other parties. This transparency is important in a way as it allows all the biases that are in the system to be found easily. In addition, making the necessary cordialities as well as responsibility, for periodically auditing and assessing the impacts, of the bias introduced AI, systems help in regulating the effects of bias in the deployed AI systems.

Together with the bias in data and algorithms, globally, specific ethical questions regarding AI are essential. So, the concept of Artificial Intelligence is not simply limited to technical products and services but analyzing its effects. This requires assessing the effects of General AI Systems on people of various categories and ensuring that their application results in similar or potentially smaller, negative or positive effects on specific categories of persons than on others. For example, when applying AI for the purpose of predictive policing, it is logical to provide information on how new tools may change police work and whether they contribute to expansion of existing prejudice in the criminal world.

Another important measure that can be connected to fair AI is the option to consider a few people's point of view regarding such AI utilization and development. That's why diverse teams are more likely to disclose bias patterns and make certain that artificial intelligence solutions were originally developed to address the needs of specific consumers. Soliciting the opinions of a particular set of end-users that are interested in implementing a particular type of AI or conversing with locals knowledgeable about the possible consequences of the AI systems can be informative in signposting how this technology can be less biase and more socially useful.

Awareness and equality are also important components that effect positive change to practical Artificial Intelligence. The people such as developers, data scientists who work in AI sector should be aware of the relevant principles of ethical approach and the necessity to combat the bias. This involves, randomness imperfection, methods used in recognition of bias and neutralizing it and the social impact of AI technologies. When the ethical aspect is rolled out into training and development, then people are able to champion moralistic AI technologies.

Therefore, and in conclusion, it could be argued that in respect of the decisions made AI can only ever become more fairly constructed as the pursuit of the respective forms of fairness is a journey. It involves an on-going scrutiny with society and tests to see if the system has regressed or shifted to a higher level of unethical behavior. Hence, whenever new styles of AI technologies are being created and introduced to the world and various fields, the issue of decreasing bias and enhancing fairness will always remain concise. Because these areas matter and should be discussed along with the problems of developing adequate kinds of AI, there is still the chance to work on the creation of new kinds of AI-equipped systems that will be equally both useful and fair.

Prejudice and justice are something one cannot ignore and cannot improve at the same time. These concerns are all the more critical because they indicate that AI is not only reproducing and increasing biases, weaknesses and unfairness but is doing so in ways that are exacerbated at each stage of AI's life cycle: from data acquisition to deployment. While being transparent, accountable, and plural, and while cultivating an ethical culture for the creation of AI technologies, we should work in the direction of raising an ethically just society. So, the struggle for fairness in AI is ongoing and despite the fact that with current work being done by all stakeholders, the work towards the further improvement of the AI fairness is accomplished.

9.2 Privacy and Data Security

Data and information privacy is very important in the present-day world where people's private information is gathered, stored and utilized by different technology machines. With the world getting more connected than ever, this has been one of the most important topics, from people's rights to organizations and even governments. This is helpful in an effort to avert scenarios that would make people lose confidence in such organizations or even get their data exploited by somebody.

Data privacy and security involve the management of other people's details to ensure that their sharing without consent becomes impossible. With the rise of digital technologies, we create and collect an ever-growing amount of personal information that might include things like browsing history, transactions, health records, messages, and more. Some of the possible uses for this sort of data include to enhance services offered, or for targeted marketing while the potential dangers incorporated in this sort of data usage are numerous only if the data is not adequately secured. Individuals' rights have been violated through identity theft personal losses and many other harms that's why security has to be strong and tight.

Another crucial concept connected with the protection of data is encryption – an encasing of data so that only the rightful recipient can undo the process. Encryption enables even in the situation would a message be intercepted or accessed by unauthorized individuals, then its content cannot be deciphered in any way. This technology has broadly been employed in preventing leakage of data during transfer for example in areas such as internet banking and emails. Moreover, there is a possibility to apply encryption when data is idle, for instance, the information that is in the hard disk or in the cloud is also protected from unauthorized use.

Another consideration is the variable of access control in the formula for data security consideration. Such controls define which users are able to view certain data and what operations are permitted with this data. Other measures include the use of better passwords, user accounts, passing nodes, and objects, the use of MFA, or authentication measures that need user to prove his/her identity more than once. It is very important: to change passwords frequently, to analyses logs and finally, to limit access for the employees who do not need it.

Various data protection laws serve important functions of prescribing how personal data ought to be processed and protected. Different countries around the world have passed legislation that provide for legal provisions on privacy in the use of data. For instance, permission for collection of data and use of the same was enhanced through the General Data Protection Regulation adopted in the EU with an aim of offering high level of protection in the data and the following rights of the citizens were granted; right in data portability, the right to access, right to be forgotten and right not to be subjected to processing. Similarly, the CCPA makes provisions for an individual's right to his or her personal information in a similar vein to the GDPR by providing the residents of California the right to opt out from data sales and request data collected on them. In this case, organizations need to adhere to these regulations to prevent legal consequence as well as to gain the trust of the users.

Still, much of data privacy and security continues to be problematic due to the following regulation hurdles. There are several barriers for example, managing numerous data sets across given systems and platforms is a challenge. When organizations are using cloud services and other forms of digital solutions the standardization of data management becomes more challenging. Trust in data management is still questionable, risks like data leaks, hackers are still present and continue to pose a constant danger as the criminals explore new ways of infiltrating secured data. To avoid these risks, environment has to be checked frequently, security improved and organizational members have to be trained on how to protect information.

Some of challenges that may arise in this case include the question of how to collect, measure and analyze information, and matters of confidentiality. Several technologies leverage data to enable customized interactions and experiences, but, the collection of this data poses questions of privacy where the process is not regulated competently and with integrity. Such findings indicate that the balance between organizational and individual interests can be achieved through the privacy by design concepts, whereby privacy concerns are addressed right from the design phase of systems in use. Clear policies concerning privacy, different possibilities to manage data, and the restriction of data processing are the counteractions for these problems.

With as advent of some new technologies for example AI, the IoT means that privacy and data security become even more complicated. Based on their logical capacity and algorithmic operations, such systems rely on the availability of considerable volumes of data, thus eliciting concerns on the acquisition, application, and dissemination of data. Because IoT devices are now being incorporated into practically all the items we use, they are capable of feeding information which may contain the basic fabric of people's activities and spaces, to central points in real-time. For this reason, such devices as well as information collected by them must be shielded to avoid such kind of experience and misuse in future.

Privacy and data security also include having obsession/training and making the staff aware at all times of the consequences regarding the issue. The rights of patients should become known to all as well as the ways in which their personal information will be protected. Protection of data includes choosing it as one of the strategic objectives of the organization and providing regular training to employees. Thus, working on creating the effective culture of protecting data, people and companies can improve the protection of personal information in the world.

the freedom and security of data are one of the norms which are highly important of achieving reliability and personal information security in the modern world of computer science. Encryption and access control are relevant since they ensure a person's data is protected from the attacker or any other unauthorized individuals. Privacy regulations must be followed, and issues regarding processing and utilization of data, as well as concerning the new technologies have to be met to guarantee the proper handling of data. This is actually the possible way on how the individuals and organizations can come hand in hand on enhancing development and promotion of privacy and security in digital environment. The question of privacy and data security is a dynamic one and hence pervious sustainable efforts will be required to effectively and efficiently counter the emerging threats and challenges.

9.3 Explainability and Transparency

AI decision-making and self-explanation transparency are crucial since they contribute to trust an accountability as well as increasing the understanding of decision-making processes. As it is identified that people require interpreting and analyzing how AI solutions work since it has been integrated into the various facets of human life, be it health, or finance sectors. This is mainly because such applications have dire implications on individuals and societal welfare.

In other words, Explainability is the ability of the members of the human society to comprehend the internal functioning of the Artificial Intelligent system in question. It covers the process of bringing the decision-making facts of the AI models to a level that is understandable. AI systems in organizations have often been developed based on very elaborate techniques such as deep learning, which are significantly hard to decode and interpret; the decision-making process therefore can be highly obscure and often referred to as having been made by a 'black box'. This opacity is a disadvantage because it becomes hard to explain why certain decisions were made or where prejudicial influences may be at work, or how the boards' outputs are fair and accurate.

While accountability refers to the proactivity in which the precise details about the operation of an AI system covering the data it relies on, the algorithms used, as well as the parameters conditioning its decisions are disclosed. Some AI is designed to include additional uncover insights behind their outputs and decisions, allowing users and stakeholders to assess the credibility of an AI system more effectively.

Another major reason for calling for explainability and transparency there is to have a guarantee that the systems are free from bias. When AI models fail to explain how they make decisions, it is almost impossible to see where the biases present within the system are. For instance, if an AI system designed for use in employment discriminates against some people in specific groups, it becomes quite challenging to understand why such discimations has happened due to the lack of explainability in such AI systems. If the decision-making process is therefore made more articulated, then it becomes easier to realize the problems and thus the way can be made free for fairness and equity for use of artificial intelligence.

Furthermore, explainability as well as transparency also play an essential role in questions of regulation and responsibility. Since AI systems are becoming regulated and standardized especially in the EU via the GDPR, organizations need to be able to provide accountability as to how the AI systems make decisions, as well as how personal data is processed. For example, under GDPR it is allowable for data subjects to have information on how decisions regarding them are made through the use of algorithms. Obeying such regulations information that organizations should incorporate explainable AI practices to so that they can cease legal and ethical requirements.

Creating explainable and transparent AI solutions by definition implies the use of different methods and strategies. The first way of developing easy to interpret models is to employ machine learning algorithms that are less opaque to comprehension than deeper ones. For instance, models from classical models set, e.g., decision trees or linear regression, are less opaque than deep neural networks. Although these models may not perform as well as more complicated equation, they are better at providing end-user insight into the decision-making process.

The third classification type is post-hoc interpretability that includes the interpretation of the models' outputs rather than the approach for developing them. Among the techniques, some of them are; feature importance, LIME, and SHAP to explain the effect that a given feature or data instance has on the classification of a given model. Such methods prove useful for interpreting the behavior of nontransparent black-box models, and therefore, they help users gain insights into what has influenced the system.

But there is more to it, and hence, the need to engage the stakeholders to ensure that they understand and contribute to the creation and assessment of explainability and transparency of the AI systems. It can be useful to involve end-users and specialists of a definite domain, or the communities affected by the AI systems and obtain their feedbacks regarding which aspects of the AI-based system need to be explained, and how this may be achieved. This means that it is easier to come up with explanations that would make sense and be useful to anybody who in one way or the other comes into contact with the given AI system.

The question of explainability and transparency also leads to enhancing such factors as users' confidence when using various AI technologies. Whenever the users understand how these AI systems make choices or decisions and see the reasoning behind the outputs then they are more likely to rely on those systems. It also indicates that with an open AI procedure, the users will make the right choices in the given situations and attempt to change or appeal the results they deem unfair or incorrect.

However, explainability and transparency have challenges that are associated with their implementation as well. It also poses as to what extent does a large model converge this predictive power where the task at hand is to design a good interpreter model. Easy ones which are easy to implement maybe and might not gain very high accuracy and the hard ones which are accurate but hard to comprehend. Most metrics that are on one side of the spectrum are usually on the opposite side of the other metrics, thus, striking a balance between accuracy and explainability depends on the application, users' needs and stakeholder needs.

An additional problem is to make these explanations not only comprehensible for AI but also reasonable for the users, to interpret it properly. The paramount aim of transparency is negated when explanations offered are technical or abstruse for interpretation by laymen. Understanding what kind of information, a particular audience requires in order to understand an explanation is key to creating such kinds of explanations.

were identified as important to make AI systems understandable to the user and make them clear for the improvement of their fairness, accountability and trustworthiness. Therefore, if the Artificial Intelligence model has more explainable decision-making criteria, and gives out the right information on how it operates, we are in a position to phase out bias, uphold the Laws and thereby be credible. The following are some of the methods of achieving these goals: interpretable models, post computational interpretability and stakeholders' involvement in model developing. Nonetheless, there are certain questions left which, owing to the interference of explainability and transparency aspects, will create a foundation for the improved and more responsible using of AI Technologies for the benefit of people and society.

9.4 Environmental Impact

The negative influence of technology on environment is an important issue today with rapid increase of the electronic and computerized equipment. From the energy expenditure used in powering data centers to disposal of electronic waste, technology has a very large ecological impact. The following are observed impacts that defining, measuring, and connecting to individual and societal well-being are important as we progressively move into the era of intensified digital transformation:

Currently, one of the most apparent threats resulting from technological advancement is energy use. Cloud computing, which is the basis of most online services and applications runs data centers that require hefty power input to power and cool servers. Increased power consumption of the data centers is ascribed to cloud services, big data, and virtual intelligence services. Such facilities are commonly reliant on fossil energy sources which in turn cause emissions of greenhouse gases and climate change. To reduce these effects organizational measures are as follows; enhanced cooling technologies, efficient computation technologies, and change of energy sources to the cleaner ones. More and more enterprises are making contractual pledges to buy green energy, or otherwise integrating practices that minimize their impact on climate, but there is still a long road to sustainability.

Flatulence of these gadgets also implies a lot of environmental impacts in productive and disposal moments. The procuring of the different materials used in manufacturing smartphones, computers and other electronics has adverse impacts on the environment and lead to pollution. Mining causes deforestation and loss of homes by animals as well as pollutes water sources and speeds up the process of terrains erosion. However, it is also pertinent to establish that most productions utilize chemical at some or the other production phase and these chemicals are mostly disastrous for the environment. When these electronic devices hit the dumping bin, they become what is referred to as e-waste, which is another problem in as far as the environment is concerned. E-waste consists of several metals that are regarded as valuable while other e-waste contains lethal materials like lead, mercury and cadmium if not disposed of properly it pollutes soils as well as the water systems.

For this reason, there is need for policies and programs on the reuse and proper disposed of electronic wastes. Some firms and some governments are now using e-waste recycling schemes to recover the useful products it contains as well as soften the impacts of these on the environment. Consumer electronics are also being produced specific to be friendly to the environment and the recycling technologies for e-waste are improving. Further, through repair, refurbishment, and reuse, the circular economy idea of how companies can reduce the need for fresh raw materials and reduce waste is slowly taking root.

It means that an evaluation of the environmental footprint of technology is not only based on the occupation of a particular space but also the use of raw materials; scope of software; and, digital services. More specifically, people consume streaming services, video gaming and other digital content, which means that they need to transfer and store data that, in turn, is due to the centers' energy consumption. In these services, there is great value in terms of ease and enjoyment, but there are also questions about how these benefit the sustainability cause. Making this service take less energy is an essential feature of addressing negative effects on the environment, which can be reached by improving algorithms and data managing.

Also, given the rate of evolution of different technologies on the market, there is something known as the 'planned obsolescence where the appliances are intentionally made with a limited lifespan and thus the owners are urged to acquire a new product after sometime. This not only ensures that the volumes of e-waste are higher, but also raises resource demand for new gadgets' manufacture. Understanding and addressing the mechanics of this progression is necessary to fight this trend and promote longer lasting products and better designed for longevity.

Measures that prevent or reduce the effects of technologies on the environment also includes encouraging proper conduct of business amongst technological companies. This year saw a surge of companies in the tech industry coming up with strategies aimed at decreasing their carbon footprint, or increasing the energy efficiency of their technologies, and using sustainable materials. As a result, the technology industry has to incorporate green production techniques; it has to fund sustainable energy and be environment-conscious. Also, joint efforts made by other stakeholders within the industry, governments, and environmental organizations enable making more coordinated system changes and therefore, aimed to offer more effective solutions to mitigate various environmental concerns that are linked to technology.

Consumer awareness and behavior also dictate the effect of technologies on the environment to a very large extent. Informing the consumer about the consequences of his/her choice on the environment, as well the persuading to consume responsibly might help to bring more moderate using devices. For example, selecting energy-saving appliances, purchasing shares in environmentally friendly oriented firms, and collecting recyclable items will reduce the offenders of ecological degradation through technology.

technology on the environment is not a simple question which covers many aspects such as energy, resources, e-waste and digital services idea of technology on the environment. These are best solved by transition strategies such as better technological approaches, improvements in mechanisms of recycling and waste management, and changes of habits among consumers. In this respect, applying sustainable strategies in the growth of the technology sector, individuals would help make the future successful and sustainable. There are many unresolved problems in connection with the existing technological innovations but environmental issues should not be less important or ignored as we address these problems in the future.

9.5 Regulatory and Legal Issues

By now, regulatory and legal questions of technology including artificial intelligence (AI) and embedded systems continue to progress as these tools continue being developed and incorporated into numerous aspects. With the recent growth of AI systems and embedded technology applications, different legal and regulating questions appear which need to be solved to prevent from unfavorable consequences.

These include issues to do with data, patent rights, and responsibility as well as changes in standards and laws.

The first regulation that arises is data protection and the second significant regulation is privacy. Since AI systems and specifically embedded devices gather and analyze personal and sensitive information, they follow several protective measures meant to ensure personal data protection. For example, the General Data Protection Regulation (GDPR) of EU provides difficult requirements concerning personal data processing. Companies are obliged to receive consent from individuals before collecting data; explain how the information will be used and give individuals control over correcting, erasing or accessing those data. Like the GDPR, other jurisdictions and countries including the state of California in the United States by the California Consumer Privacy Act (CCPA) control the processing of personal information by technology firms. Some of these aspects should be well selected as well as the methods used in implementing them should include measures in the prevention of loss of data.

Another important regulatory problem relates to the issues of intellectual property (IP) rights. It is important that with time, and advancement in the use of technology especially, the aspect of IP is protected to encourage developers as well as creators to get credit for their endeavors. AI and embedded systems can be integrated by secret algorithms, software and specific hardware structures that must be protected by patents, copyrights, and other types of secrets. However, the rate of advancement in this area opens opportunity for chances for IP ownership and infringement disputes. There is a shift needed towards standards and legal boundaries and parameters regarding IP so as to support growth of new invention while creating competition and collaboration at the same time.

Increasing one's roles, Responsibility in artificial intelligence for decision-making is becoming an issue since the systems are more expansive and independent. Due to the vast effect of AI systems that imposes potentials harm to the individual and society, there is a need to enforce clear responsibility arrangements. Holding an AI system and thus responsible for its action, let alone if those decisions affect other people's lives has become very complex. These areas legally demand answers to questions of who is liable or accountable should an AI system provide a wrongly derived decision, or worse still, lead to an incurring of a loss. This implies what every developer, user and any other party affiliated with the use of AI must do to enhance the safety, ethical and legal usage of the technology.

Another difficulty in management of risks is that an organization has to adapt to current standards or required regulations. With technology, advancing every day, institutions strive to meet and establish new sets of measures to solve arising questions. Such changes must be followed by these organizations when ordering technologies and the latter must conform to the existing legislation. This covers regulation of data protection and protection of intellectual property rights, safety and security of use as well as ethical use in some industries. For instance, self-driving cars, medical equipment and appliances are regulated to the standard and performance requirement. Dealing with such a vast number of rules implies constant identification of shifts and finding ways not to get caught by the rules.

The second theme and relationship between ethics and technology involve regulatory and legal concerns. With growing application of AI systems and other embedded smart technologies it becomes crucial to raise ethical issues as to how these are used and with what effects. These questions include; Algorithm fairness, bias, discrimination and how such data should be handled by society? Such a question brings society to a realization that appropriate regulation of the technology for fairness and justice needs to be done. All these ethical issues call for the legal system to be fitted to the regulation of these technologies. This consist of having regulations that support policies that prohibit discrimination and ensure a gender balance in the technology industry and technology information content.

Data crossing borders and state laws and international standards form two additional layers of consideration. Many technology business organizations have their operations implemented on an international platform, meaning they have to undergo different national and global legal requirements. Because of the differences in legal requirements of many countries, there may exist inconsistencies in the protection, cybersecurity, and technology standards of the organizations that function in the global context. The challenges are in the harmonization of matters of regulations and compliance to a plethora of legal systems to govern cross-border issues affecting international business while addressing privacy of data transferred across nations.

By addressing these regulatory and legal concerns appropriately, the stakeholders will require partnership. For this reason, governments and specialized regulatory authorities, Industry professionals and technology creators MUST provide more integral and specific guidelines to the ever-changing interrelated problems of new technology. More specific than the first, do's and don'ts and fruitful discussions with other countries on the successful implementation of regulations in their jurisdictions can contribute to the emergence of appropriate legal frameworks that will support the creation of new products that are not harmful to individuals and society.

challenges examined in this paper show that regulatory and legal concerns in the context of technology, especially AI and other embedded systems, can be complex and dynamic. Privacy, piracy, responsibility, adherence to standards, and ethical issues are the fields that should be mentioned while considering significant issues. These are some of the challenges that are persisting as technology continues to enhance itself and as we look for solutions to these problems it is critical that there be defined and elastic rules to govern technology. It is necessary to matrix the rules and keep interacting with the stakeholders and using monitorship tools with the benefit of using technology to enhance good outcomes without breaching legal and ethical standards.

9.6 Best Practices for Ethical AI Development

To create ethical AI one needs some directions in order to make the technological process as close to ethical rules as possible. Such is the need for effective guidelines for appropriate AI development to address risks and contingencies associated with the increased incorporation of AI into such aspects of human life as decision making, health care, finance, and more.

One of the fundamental best practices in the creation of ethical AI is following non-bias representation. When AI systems are trained with a large set of data, and if these contain biases of different types they will reinforce them or even aggravate the same. For instance, let's imagine an AI that was trained for job applications; if the training set is unbalanced by some demographics, the AI system will continue discriminating similar applications. As to this, developers must try to use a variety of and balanced data sets, attach procedures for bias detection and mitigation in their models, and periodically review them with the aim of making models fairer. Moreover, time-to-time management of diverse employees indicates that there are prejudicial debates created during the progress of the IT system are minimized by other views.

Another element of ethical AI design include is transparency. That means the actions of the AI systems are comprehensible and visible to all and sundry. This means elaborating on issues like how the models for AI arrive at a conclusion or even what data the AI uses and ultimately, the algorithm of use. This way users trust is built since the practices are transparent and users are capable of understanding AI outputs and asking relevant questions if need be. Aid systems renew that there are more types such as explanation tools, feature importance scores, or even to explain a specific AI decision there is a method called local interpretable model-agnostic explanations (LIME). In this case, the developers can ensure that the AI systems work in an accountably manner and enable the users to trust AI systems by pushing for transparency.

Among ethical issues that relate to development of AI some of them include privacy, data protection and the following issues. One of the main goals of dealing with AI systems is that these systems handle large amounts of personal information; hence, its security is paramount. They have to follow laws like GDPR or CCPA, that are the laws that regulate how and why data could be collected, stored or used. High data protection that generates data encryption and users' rights of accessing data minimize the exposure of data and leakage. Furthermore, developers should be selective with the data they gather by being proportional by only gathering data important for the operation of the AI system and always communicating to the users in what way their data will be used.

This is considerable in the ethical AI since it defines legal resentment as well as duty of care of those developing the AI technologies and those applying the technologies. Effective reporting therefore means laying down of responsibilities whereby everyone that is involved in the AI life cycle is assigned his or her role. This also includes through which bodies the functioning of AI in terms of ethical issues is coordinated or regulated, and feedback or complaints/issue related to the functioning of the AI systems. The best way to achieve this is for developers, organizations, and policymakers to regulate and standardize on methods that will make parties responsible for their actions concerning the Executive funnel, to the letter, as well as put up channels for auditing and reviewing the process of the AI systems to ensure standards compliance.

Ethical AI development also has to be dynamic showing that is has the capability of learning and improving as time goes on. The world of technology and norms are fluid; the right thing to do may change over time. Second, developers should keep on discovering new ethical issues and decisions to expand or enhance the existing literature in this field. This involves engagements with other stakeholders in the industry, ethicists and researchers and the adoption of the feedback received from the users and other relevant stakeholders in the society. Unbalanced methods facilitate the prevention of ethical matters at an early stage, and permit developers to address enhancing their conduct based on the ethical norm.

The following are the ethical consideration: Ethical consideration: There is a corporate responsibility within organizations that develop AI applications. This involves integrating the best ethical practice into business environment and operations. In order for it to change, awareness must be created through training and education programs to developers, data scientists and other allied parties, regarding the ethics of the matter. Ethical awareness and focal encouragement enhance the ethical behavior and ethical decision-making aiding to prioritize ethical impacts within the development scenario.

Another best practice of ethical AI development is and cross-sectoral cooperation. Tackling the ethical issues arising from the use of artificial intelligence hence calls for interdisciplinary effort from technology, law and social sciences as well as philosophy. Communication with practitioners in different fields allows to consider more extensive range of effects and humanitarian aspects of the application of artificial intelligence. However, talks with other external players like the regulation agencies and the advocacy groups may assist in framing right policies and standards to be adopted in right usage of AI.

Finally, the general impact of installed AI systems for the public is an aspect under ethical considerations. There are chances that the use of AI will affect various permits of people such as employment, social relations and access to resources. The creators of AI systems should track if the ideas they are implementing have a positive impact on society or may have various negative consequences, and design such systems to bring only the benefits. On the same tone, factors such as divide, accessibility and the consequences of AI systems are taken into account.

there are several guidelines on ethical AI implementation including; two; fairness, transparency, privacy, responsibility, and reflect & improve. Hence when incorporated to develop the AI systems and when people are taken through a culture of responsibility, they can be able to develop AI with ethics that resonate with our own. Integration from interdisciplinary and multi-sector perspectives also strengthens the capacity to confront ethical issues and promote the right technological development. As AI continues to intensify and transform the future, stepping into the notion of the best practices highlighted above will be crucial to embrace if only to make the technology useful for the general public and if only to uphold the esteemed ethicality.

CHAPTER 10: FUTURE TRENDS IN EMBEDDED DEEP LEARNING AND GENERATIVE AI

10.1 Emerging Technologies

New technologies Spark new generations of industries, Economies and general existence and this has produced impressive opportunities as well as raison d'être difficulties. These technologies just like any other technologies advancing day by day in every field of life and having a potentiality to increase the productivity, to increase the quality of life, and to solve many global problems but, on the other hand, they required to handle, think carefully about them and manage properly.

The most prominent one of them all is Artificial Intelligence (AI) which is been brought up to par and is useful in many areas. AI may include, machine learning, natural language processing, robotics, and Computer vision. These technologies make computers functional in performing what was thought to be relevant to human intellect comprehending data, predicting, and even in having a conversation with the users. Industries that AI presents opportunities to revolutionize include the healthcare, AI can help in detecting diseases, treatment plans and administration. In finance, AI algorithms can even analyze the stock market, check for fraud and even determine the best way to invest. But they also raise ethical and regulatory concerns such as privacy or fairness, and questions of responsibility in the relatively new area. As such, proper assessment of risks and benefits with relevance to the implementation of artificial intelligence should be carried out for the two parties as they optimize the other's value-added systems.

One of these technologies is the blockchain and apart from the crypto-currencies such as the Bitcoin and Ethereum, it holds value. Blockchain is a modern technology that employs the use of cryptographic concepts to decentralize modes of recording and sharing data with clarity through consensus. In addition to digital currencies, the use of blockchain technology can be of particular value in supply chain where it can improve transparency and decrease fraud, as it would maintain ledgers of the kinds of transactions that took place. It also offers potential solution in such uses cases like smart contracts which is self-executed contract without third parties' intervention as well as in the decentralized finance (DeFi) that being a kind of financial revolution to decentralize financial market. Nevertheless, blockchain has some inherent issues like scalability, the high consumption of energy and also legal issues. To make this happen it is important that most of these issues are dealt with to ensure that there is proper integration of this system in many sectors.

Other emergent technologies that will allow some problems that it is currently hard for normal computers to solve are Quantum computing. Quantum computers then vary with classical computers in that the former uses quantum bits, or qubits, which exist in multiple states at once. As it happens, this capability allows quantum computers to address numerous matters vastly faster than conventional hardware; possible applications include cryptography, material science, optimization, and much else. Nonetheless, it is still in its infancy and must overcome different technical and theoretical challenges. Academician tries to search how to manipulate the qubit, debug the quantum computer and provide good algorithms for the use of quantum computer.

Internet of Things (IoT) is another technology that is slowly finding its way in aspects of daily life and business. IoT is therefore the collection of devices and sensors all connected and transmitting information over the internet. These includes smart home devices such as switches, lighting, security and even industrial apparatus such as machine tool regulating systems, among others, to monitor and control real time processes for automation. Within the context of smart cities IoT can be used to optimize traffic flows, monitor environment and maintain public order and safety. For instance, in the health sector the IoT devices can be harnessed to track patient's status and different parameters; this would result into accurate and early treatment. Still, as huge opportunities that IoT opens for the development of technologies, it opens challenges that are linked with security questions and compatibility of the devices, user's data protection. Making IoT systems reliable, safe, and easily integrable with current applications and networks is essential to making the most of connected systems.

5G is next generation connectivity that features continually improved capabilities of peak data rate, latency, and traffic capacity compared to prior mobile network generation. 5G networks are believed to unlock growth in many areas ranging from self-driving cars to AR and even remote operations like surgery. Through providing a high-level of speed and dependable connectivity of devices and networks, 5G is expected to enable launch of novel services and applications that necessitate the processing of real-time data. However, with the 5G roll out come questions around the infrastructure investment, possible health effects and the use of spectrum. Taking care of these concerns while stepping forward toward producing 5G technology is going to be significant to fully retain its utility and its integration into society.

The other industry that is also fast growing is the biotechnology and this is due to existent development in gene editing techniques, synthetic biology and that of personalized medicine. The more recent molecular procedures like the CRISPR-Cas9 which developed in the recent past made provisions for variations on the DNA strands and further has ramifications in disease eradication, crop resistance and formulation of new drugs. Some applications of biology include design and assembly of new biological components and systems, development of engineered materials and green technology. The practice that targets the delivery of medical treatments based on the patient's individual genetic makeup known as personalized medicine is set to enhance the quality of the delivered health care service and minimize on the side effects. However, they involve some loss aspects of the biotechnology concerning the liberation with ethical issues and safety of genetic management, the extent and consequences of which are repercussion and probable abuses. Therefore, the effective foundation of the COE ethical standards and legal

Wing in the use and creation of the biotechnologies is essential.

When one technology emerges, it will follow the same path of another technology offering innovative approaches to industries and societies when two or more technologies interact. Accepting such innovations while implementing solutions for the problems that come with them are most effective when undertaken in a cross-sectoral method incorporating researchers, policymakers, industry members and the public. It is imperative to duplicate the efforts for creating a culture of innovative and preventive regulation to enable and utilize technological development as a means to face the global challenges and enhance the standards of living and co development. The major challenge will be to achieve all these while considering ethic, environmental and social concerns in order to reap from these technologies in a manner that will be in the best of society and in a sustainable manner.

10.2 Advances in Hardware and Software

Innovations in the technology hardware and software are pushing the improvement of the field to increased rate by making it faster and capable of solving more complicated problems. This outcome is due to the interdependence between developments in hardware and in software which have enabled various industries to make revolutionary advancements that most probably could not have been contemplated just a generation ago. All these are occupying fields like Artificial intelligence (AI), Robotics and embedded systems among others, and is changing the way humans' interface with them.

Among the aspects of the hardware and software activity that may be characterized by rather high rates of changes is the development of specialized processing units. The primary logical processors have ever been the classical CPUs, but with the rise of the project difficulty and exponentially growing needs in AI and ML, there appeared new subtypes of the processors. GPUs are basically used for generating images which were but are used for parallel computation, which is the needed for training deep learning models. This is to mean that the GPUs are well suited for large set of data and algorithms than the CPUs this because of the computation part.

Even more specialized directions can be identified as moving further along this axis, the special built Tensor Processing Units (TPUs) and Neural Processing Units (NPUs). TPUs are known as deep learning accelerators and have been designed by Google, the chips are optimized for ML operations or more specifically, the full processes of training and implementing the machine learning models. NPUs which are available in today's smartphones and other edge devices augment AI in devices; they offer the advantage of bringing the processing to the device rather than having to drag it to the cloud with consequent burden to power. These improvements in the handling processors are crucial so that the real time applications of AI like self-driving cars and smart homes to perform seamlessly.

From the software perspective, constant growth of AI frameworks and development tools enabled developers and researchers construct and implement enhanced models. Platforms such as TensorFlow, PyTorch, and MXNet have ensured that some technologies such as machine learning and deep learning are well enhanced to users due to availing enhanced libraries and tools for model construction. These provide readymade template, optimized code and samples where lay persons too can play around with AI and work on sample scenarios for application. Specifically, TensorFlow is using actively to working well in both research and production and can be used practically in a variety of projects. While researchers prefer PyTorch for its flexibility, it is also being adopted by commercial applications because of the friendly user interface it offers and the presence of a very active community.

The other emerging software development is the advancement of edge computing platforms. Currently, with continuing expansion of the Internet of Things (IoT) devices, the necessity appears in data processing at the edge rather than centralized in cloud servers. Local computing has the advantage of replicating data processing on devices and thus cutting latency, bandwidth usage and power consumption. Machine learning promises to process data on edge devices such as smartphones, drones, and even vehicle control systems, thanks to UL's methods, frameworks like TensorFlow Lite and ONNX. This is particularly the case in uses cases such as self-driving cars where real-time control is necessary and cloud interconnectivity poses risks of time-sensitive latency.

In parallel to hardware and software developments, storage solutions are improving the management of large volumes of data. T h e traditional hard disk drive is then being substituted by the faster and more reliable solid-state drive which is permitting systems to access and store data at increased rates. As is the case with AI, where often models are trained on large sets requiring long time to access, quicker access to storage facilitates faster model development. In addition, there have been advancement in the usage of cloud base system where big data can be stored, analyzed and retrieved with lots of on-site infrastructure. Cloud based storage solutions have a high measure of scalability and flexibility so that organizations may be able to enhance storage space as required without undue concern over the amount of storage space required.

One of the most promising trends in development in both hardware and software is the increasing incorporation of AI into the design of the hardware. Hardware-aware NAS is an example of such cases where, AI is employed to search for efficient hardware implementations of different machine learning tasks. The idea results in more efficient hardware that are optimized for training AI models and improving the gap between hardware and AI models. Also, the new software tricks like quantization and pruning, in neural network optimization, help generate AI models which are lighter and can run on less hardware intensive devices. These methods are very important in the deployment of AI in eedevies seeing that power and computational capabilities are constrained.

This is similarly observed in the increasing subfields of autonomous systems, such as robotics or self-driving cars that advance both in hardware and software with each year. Sensor advances like LiDAR and radar also supplemented with sophisticated AI algorithms enable the autonomous system to sense the environment much more accurately and respond to it immediately. The capabilities of various high-performance hardware, for example, GPU, TPU, allow these systems to analyze large amounts of sensor data and make complex decisions at the same time. Overall, there has been a progressive enhancement of both the hardware and software support of autonomous systems to function in dynamic environment and to execute tasks for higher precision and self-sufficiency.

Besides robotics, the healthcare sector is proving that innovation prevails as a growing number of improvements in both hardware and software emerge. New models of portable and wearable apparatuses imply medical devices which contain complicated artificial intelligence systems to measure the patient's vital signs, observe changes, and determine the future physiological state of the patient based on prior information. Recent research has also revealed that improved imaging systems, meaning MRI and CT scans and systemized artificial intelligence diagnostics, are helping medical practitioners as well to diagnose diseases earlier and more accurately. The emergence of application specific integrated circuits/ system on chip/reference signal generator for medical applications along with intelligent algorithm for data processing and control is proving to be a growth avenue in fields of precision medicine, health tele monitoring, and surgical assistant.

the daily advancements in both hardware and software are making it easier to bring revolutionary changes in various sectors. Firstly, non-necessity of traditional GPU for specialized, novel processing units for specific devices and edge-computing platforms and updated frameworks in artificial intelligence processing result in the expansion of possible further advancements in fields of artificial intelligence systems, robotics, healthcare and automobiles. Given these technologies advances in the future the hardware and software meld will become the primary driver of more beneficial, smarter, and capable systems that will revolutionize the life, work, and interaction with the environment.

10.3 Integration with Other Technologies: Blockchain, 5G, Quantum Computing

This is due to increase adoption of new technologies such as blockchain, 5G and quantum computing, whereby there is large innovation in various fields that provide options to revolutionize paradigms. These technologies help enable distinct features, and, when integrated, complement each other's prowess in ways that could spark innovation to heights unknown.

Promising to maintain decentralization and security, blockchain can increasingly enter into other technologies as an enabler of their performance and credibility. In simple terms, blockchain is a real-time and easily-shared record of exchange of value that is secure due to decentralization. The characteristic is most useful when used together with other technologies that require the swapping of trustworthy data. For instance, in the case of IoT, using blockchain can resolve concerns to do with accuracy and credibility of data. IoT devices create a massive amount of data that is prone to be forged or corrupted. Instead, with blockchain, managers or owners of organizations can establish a strong record system of data transactions, which guarantees the received and collected data from IoT devices to be credible. While improving the IoT security it also brings more transparency and performance to such fields as SCM, smart contracts, etc.

There is another promising case – Blockchain integrated with 5G: 5G is the new generation of mobile communications that has Higher data rate, Lower latency, and Higher connection density. Adding 5G into the blockchain can expand the approach to provide better security as well as reliability of distributed nets. For instance, blockchain application that can improve the security of the 5G network depends on the enormous amount of data that such a network processes, by creating a distributed ledger for the same. It can also improve the security of exchanging information between devices, by increasing the protection of data privacy. Moreover, blockchain presents opportunities in providing secure and efficient transactional platforms that are timely given the low latency offered by 5G networks for connected cars, smart buildings and remote health care providers respectively.

On its own, quantum computing can solve problems that are challenging for a classical computer and, when integrated with blockchain and 5G, poses even higher capability. The core business of quantum computing including data processing and pile calculations that can actually offer revolutionary results in cybersecurity and cryptography. Quantum computing can be employed for advancements in the concept of blockchain in which data has to be protected by employing definite cryptographic methods. Several cryptographic solutions are still being designed to protect blockchain networks against quantum threat in the advent of future quantum threats.

Also, when deployed concurrently with the quantum computing, 5G networks have benefits for telecommunication systems through the improvement of performance and the security levels. To them, quantum computing can enhance 5G networks by optimizing the complicate network algorithms and enhancing signal processing due to its high efficiency and reliability. On a broader perspective, the integration of quantum algorithms can help in efficient utilization of resource of the network; efficient routing of data; making the link availability of 5G much more reliable across varied applications leading to seamless and reliable communication. Also, the use of quantum encryption method can improve reliability of data that is transmitted through 5G networks since it focuses on issues to do with data leakage and keep sensitive information secure.

Blockchain in combination with 5G and quantum computing also creates brand-new opportunities in such sectors as the financial industry, healthcare, and logistics. In the financial sector specifically, the combination of these technologies would likely result in the creation of better protection for their transactions, smart contracts, And their financial data integrity systems. For example, blockchain can also facilitate decentralized storing of digital currencies and energies, while 5G expedites reliable transactions. Machine learning can improve the analytical foundations of finance and business, design and evaluate investment portfolios more effectively.

In healthcare, the applications of these technologies can bring innovation for the best solutions of personalized medicine, remote health analysis and even medical experimentation. Blockchain can encode and interface PII while keeping it private and creating interoperability between healthcare facilities; 5G can enable mobility and quick transfer of large image data; and quantum computing can model drug or genomic analysis using big data sets and modeling. Combined, they may bring improvements to healthcare delivery; therefore, making the healthcare system to be efficient in the way patients are treated.

Blockchain, 5G and quantum computing in the logistics and supply chain industry can lead to huge changes in how the tracking and distribution of goods is carried out. Blockchain technology will help verify and track the origin and legitimacy of products through an open and permanent ledger while 5G will enhance real-time control over the product and its movements and quantum will help the chain to maneuver and find and solve problems that it comes across during the process. This integration can result into effective and flexible supply chain, decreased cost, better communication and thus result to better customer experience.

Over time, these tertiary technologies will further develop and interlink therefore pose significant factors in dictating the provision of different forms of industries. The integration of blockchain, 5G, and quantum computing offers a perfect storm of defining technological breakthrough of the next decade and solve some of the most challenging problems that society faces. However, realizing the full potential of these technologies is a challenging question that scientists, developers, and industry partners have to solve to overcome the technological barriers, ensure compatibility of the solutions proposed, and create effective tools to fit various applications.

blockchain as part of emerging technologies tackle with the synergy of 5G and quantum computing as some of the major disruptive point solutions in various fields. When combined, the innovative aspects of each technology can be used to develop systems that are more secure, operate at higher efficiency, and have increased capability to change industries and raise the standard of living. Further developments of these technologies and attempts to implement them into solutions will be seen as prerequisite in providing stability to their applications and for addressing the remaining potentials of information age.

10.4 The Role of AI in Shaping the Future

Artificial Intelligence which a few years ago was viewed as a great idea for the future has become a practical worldview, an instrument for transforming various industries and the world in general. With advancements in the generation of technologies in AI, much more is being expected from them in terms of how they will influence various sectors in the future depending with the existing ideas as applied in medical facility, business field, mechanical sector, teaching fraternity and even learning institutions. AI is not only the automation tool; it's a disruptive technology that changes the very fabric of our existence.

Probably the most profound area where AI is pointing to is the future that the capability of solving tasks that involving intelligent human effort autonomously. It is rather well-known in sectors like manufacturing in which robotic structures as well as

AI machines perform better in repetitive actions than humans. But now AI is starting to progress from the kind of work previously handled by basic manufacturing robots to more cognitively demanding types of work including data analysis, decision-making, and even creative work. In finance for example, artificial intelligence algorithms are being employed predictive analytics, risk assessment, and decision making of investments. Such capabilities not only enhance productivity but also back up decision making processes within the organizations with relevant data.

Today AI is also driving the change in nearly all facets of healthcare including diagnosis precision, individual approach to patients, and drug development speed. What AI – created by applying machine learning algorithms to large datasets of medical records – might capture that clinicians themselves may overlook? For example, AI systems are used in the diagnosing of illnesses; identification of early symptoms of diseases including cancer, achievable through examination of X-ray images and MRIs. Similarly, the AI application on Personalized medicine has helped doctors to deliver customized wants and needs of personal patients through genetics, inverse, and record. Such an approach is enhancing the quality of patient care and minimizing the error-prone approach that conventional methods entail.

Another of the focused areas is also for transport through utilization of autonomous cars and other related smart transport technologies. As many self-driving vehicles are already developed with the help of AI, it becomes possible to predict the future of transportation as safer, more effective and available to a greater number of people. Car autonomics uses a number of sensors, cameras and other machine learning that enables the car to understand its environment, and come up with a strategy on what to do to avoid a certain obstacle or to go around it.

As it can be observed, with enhancement of this technology, occurrences of traffic accidents resulting from human factors, fuel usage and congestion in urban areas can in a big way be minimized. Besides, the transport industry is embracing AI in planning the best routes in transport networks, cutting the time passengers have to spend waiting for the services, and enhancing their experience.

AI has a whole lot that it will positively affect in the future and education is one area that AI cannot be left out. It has already made its way in customizing learning experiences, delivering content based on the learner, or providing feedback immediately. These technologies are increasing the chances for student in enabling the learner from any background to learn in their own stratum and also are given individual consideration. Nevertheless, lessons are also helpful for an AI as it contributes to educators by minimizing administrative work including grading, attendance and so on, so that the teacher will be able to dedicate his/ her time with the students and making them creative. As AI progresses it is expected that the education model will slowly be adapted making learning more flexible, engaging and student centered.

In the sphere of commerce and industry, therefore, AI is bringing valuable enhancements in efficiency and creativity. Real-world examples show that AI is being applied on supply chain management, customer services and many other areas to improve organizational performance. For example, in retail, AI deals with data such as customers' behaviors, patterns and buying preferences to enhance marketing vendue and customer experiences. Most of AI that has already integrated into business environments help to improve customer support, answer clients' inquiries 24/7 online. In manufacturing, for example, AI derived predictive maintenance systems are cutting on downtime by pointing at likely equipment failure beforehand. Not only are these costs prevented but also the operating efficiency of the enterprise is improved.

Science and research are another area in which AI is playing an enormously significant role as the future maker. AI is applied by scientists in data processing in hypothesis development and in the advancement of knowledge in areas such as physics, biology, chemistry among others. For instance, deep learning is applied to model molecular behavior with the aim of discovering new drugs, and other materials. This is done to identify objects within an astronomical telescope and to enable astrophysics to solve some of the challenges of the universe through analysis of large data sets with the aid of Artificial Intelligence. These are not only exciting innovations as to the extension of human knowledge but as to opportunity for addressing many of the world's most significant problems, including global warming, health, and energy.

However, as the development of AI moves forward, more global ethical and social concerns come up as trends. AI is gradually being taken into companies and organizations and this leaves a chance to disrupt markets as people are fired by computers. AI brings new opportunities, and new jobs, thus triggering the need for new employees' skills at the same time. This leads to problems of job automation and the problem of whether workers can afford to be trained to fit into the new job market facilitated by artificial intelligence. Moreover, decision making by AI — whether in fields of health or finance, law enforcement or justice — has raised debate issues of transparency, decisional accountability and last not least bias. To ensure that the uses are fair and not prejudiced those proposing the development of such technologies will need to follow carefully to reduce negative impacts.

However, the use of AI is not devoid of some concerns, particularly with reference to one's privacy. Most AI solutions essentially gather large amounts of personal information to perform processes and the process of data gathering and utilization must follow the rules of protecting the individual's data privacy. Since some of the data to be analyzed in the AI systems may include personally identifiable information or health, financial records, etc., the AI systems must be secure enough to avoid being hacked. In addition, there is a discus-HHEM 342 sion on the ethical position of the artificial intelligence in relation to the surveillance technologies systems which are positioned to spy on a person without the knowledge or consent of the person in question.

Thus, AI will continue to be one of the important dynamic future forces and help to address world issues. AI will also enable real societal impact and contribution to positive social change from fighting climate change to the availability of health care in regions that have little access. These objectives however cannot and should not be attained in this manner without prudent and selective approach to the development of cort Antarctica's /AI systems which is also equally relevant to contemplate the ethos and society impact on the society and mankind in general.

Hence, the future was expected to be shaped by AI in a vast, multi-faceted and to a significant extent diverse way. AI means growth and development that it came with its ability to automate processes, enhance decision making and spur innovation that is transforming industries today. That is why the further development of the AI concept cannot be viewed exclusively as a spontaneous recognition of opportunities that can be found in the possibility of creating intelligent machines. This way we'll be ensuring that AI is for improving the quality of life on this planet and is making the future of this world better.

10.5 Predictions and Speculations

With AI and other new generation technologies – not to mention the Internet of Things – advancing with lightning speed, expectations and forecasts concerning the future role of these technologies enter an ever more fascinating realm. AI, machine and deep learning, robotics, and now quantum computing are the four that are expected to recast many industries, economies, societies, and cultures. Some are looking at the 'positive effects'; viz enhanced quality of life, enhanced productivity and better solutions to complex scientific problems many are addressing negatives such as loss of employment, ethical dilemmas and potential negative advances with ever emerging autonomous systems. By detailing out both cases we get to hope not only on the fantastic future to come but also on the challenges that come with an AI society.

Of these the most common mention is about AI's ability to participate or interface in every area of human endeavor, including personalized medical treatment of diseases, fully autonomous cars. In healthcare AI is already useful as an analytical tool, for diagnosing illnesses and suggesting courses of treatment. Their expectation is that as software and artificial intelligence advance, they will be able to execute operations, design medication according to a patient's genes, as well as track the health trends of the population to eradicate outbreaks of diseases. These could extend increased life expectancy and quality living but they would continue to raise others technical moral issues more especially concerning privacy of data and choices in critical life situations.

Future realism has the potential to render the human driver completely redundant in the light of self-driving cars and delivery drones, not to mention the potential for Artificial Intelligence to managing public transport systems. Such automobiles are controlled by elaborate software technologies, and this makes them safe from accidents than being operated by people. Logistics networks using AI could transform the supply forwards chain, sutatially decreasing delivery times whilst increasing the efficiency of global trade. However, the following question arises to ask on how these existing industries for instance the trucking industry, the taxi services or even the airline industries will progressively change to adapt to the advancement. One might be job loss, which can be a huge result, but societies will have to answer as to how they will retool workers and reshape economies in relation to such development.

AI is also, expected to assume a significant role in solving environmental issues especially through efficient resource utilization. For example, in agricultural sector, artificial intelligence can assist farmers to check crop status and estimated yield, minimize water and pesticides use and hence increase on farming efficiency. Better regulation of these energy demands could be accomplished autonomously by the use of artificial intelligence and help further advance ways for energy savings with using wind and other natural resources. In addition, climate models developed by AI could add to the current knowledge about climate change and provide users with better predictions for the future, which would help to make changes to the global climate policy. They have the potential of reducing quantum of harms caused to the environment as a result of activities carried out by the inhabitants of this planet but varies with political will and more so international cooperation.

One area where one is most likely to find AI predictions a plenty is in scientific research. Giving a new dimension to various sectors quantum computing along with the field of AI is likely to open several doors in various scientific branches including the biology, physics, chemistry etc. These technologies could lead to faster progress in bringing new drugs to market, accurately solve mathematical problems that heretofore could not be solved, and model molecular behavior in order to design novel materials. Most people have been led to believe that AI will help scientists crack problems that can lead to the further discovery of fundamental parts of the universe such as the cradle of life. We still have to ask the philosophical question: But how far can discovery go if guided by AI? Will AI provide us with something that our ancestors failed to comprehend for centuries or will it show us boundaries that cannot be crossed?

When it comes to the workforce, discourse tends to center on automation that brought with it an assumption that AI would provide solutions and phases out human labor throughout various sectors. What proof exists for the central characteristic of jobs that are at risk of being automated is that they consist of low variability, simple, standardized, routine tasks? The change according to some theorists will extend to a future where AI and robotics have radically transformed the nature of work eradicating most presently existing forms of work, and replacing them with communal work that is centered on creativity, problem-solving, and personal interaction. Some people assume that AI will only deepen inequality because while employees in engineering, IT, etc., are going to be in high demands, those at the bottom will not have that kind of prospects. To avoid these risks, most foresee those conditions like universal basic income, widespread retraining exercises, and overhauls of education systems to prepare the generations to come for an AI-led tomorrow will be requiring.

That is why the ethical implications of the further development of AI are one more active topic of discussion. Insert The more the technology advances and incorporate into decision-making frameworks in healthcare, law enforcement or governance contexts the more the issues such as bias, opacity and accountability becomes an issue. Today, some people believe that soon machines could start to make decisions with the least amount of intervention from humans, which leads to the following questions of how to shape these systems to be pro-social. There are also similar, well-founded apprehensions pertaining to development of autonomous weaponry and the possibility of setting war by machines and not by humans. Such scenarios have now allowed some people to call for the slowing down of development or an outright ban in branches that may be detrimental to human rights and global security.

Another aspect of discussion that concerns AI is certainly the potential part that it plays in creativity. With the advancement of technology in AI systems there is always the question, that with increased capability of creating art, music, literature, and other literary forms the AI systems pose to human creativity. Could AI work as the extension of mannerism that supplies artists new tools to develop their arts, art pieces; or could it replace human creativeness eventually? Most of the experts believe that a time will come when an AI will deliver pieces of work that are unique and maybe even better than works produced by man, meaning our perception of creativity will evolve. Some people continue arguing that AI can reproduce various aspects and attributes of creativity but it cannot capture profound emotions that form human sensation which serve as the essence of great art.

The richest conjuncture ideas, which may be considered as the most futuristic, concern the idea of developing general intelligence of AI, the machines that would be able to think, reason, and learn as general as a particular human example. At the present moment, the practical AI can be viewed as highly specialized and quite restricted in the number of tasks it is able to solve, but there is a concept of artificial general intelligence, or AGI. Some say that creation of an AGI could possibly happen within the next few decades, and from this AI systems with human level or greater cognition would arise. What AGI will mean is inspiring and terrifying at the same time. On one hand, the capability of AGI can for some of humankind's greatest problems such as disease and space travel. While it boosts efficiency, it raises existential risks as machines that have evolved to be smarter than human beings do tasks in strange or dangerous ways that are hazardous to human beings.

the prospect for AI is rife with both untapped potential and major problems. As to the extent of its effect, much can be said and done, the general consensus is that AI will continue to leave an indelible mark in the manner by which it transforms industries and societies and interacts with individuals. Whether the future will be one of technological advancement and growth, where organizations and their customers and citizens will flourish is down to our specific choices when it comes to how to develop and deploy AI-related technologies and how to govern them both internationally and locally. We can only make educated guesses about the future direction but the role that AI will play in the future is not in doubt.

www.ingramcontent.com/pod-product-compliance
Lightning Source LLC
LaVergne TN
LVHW022332060326
832902LV00022B/3997